It's All in the Bag!

A Whole-Language Approach to Introducing the Alphabet and Letter/Sound Recognition

by Gloria Mehrens and Karen Wick

Fearon Teacher Aids

Simon & Schuster Supplementary Education Group

Acknowledgments

To Victor H. Dickinson, principal, Emerson
Elementary School, who gave us the freedom to
be creative.
To the children of Emerson, whose
enthusiasm enabled us to carry on.
To the educators at Emerson, who encouraged us
to share our program.
To all the educators who have gone before us and
with us and especially to Bob and Marlene
McCracken, whose inspiration was
invaluable.
To George F. Mehrens, Jr., who was our
severest critic and support system
through it all.
To Ina V. Tabibian, who made it all possible.
We say thank-you!

Editor: Carol Williams
Copyeditor: Cynthia Seagren
Design: Walt Shelly
Illustrations created by Gloria Mehrens and Karen Wick
and redrawn by Duane Bibby.

ISBN 0-8224-6451-9

Printed in the United States of America
1. 9 8 7 6 5 4 3

Contents

Introduction

It's All in the Bag! provides you with a multitude of activities to help you build a strong letter/sound recognition program. Refer to the weekly lesson guide on page 6 for a basic format to follow. Supplement this basic format with activities from the "Special Activities" page for each specific sound. And, choose additional activities from pages 7–9 that can be used with any letter or sound. Choose several activities weekly from each of these three pages (Classwork, Seatwork, Homework) to meet the needs of your students.

The "Special Activities" pages include music, language arts, cooking, handwriting, math, science, and art activities. Each handwriting activity includes a "silly sentence" that contains words beginning with the sound of the week. Write the sentence on the chalkboard or chart. Then have students copy it onto paper and illustrate it. A reproducible worksheet is also included with each sound for students to practice writing uppercase and lowercase letters and to stimulate vocabulary development.

It is often suggested in the "Special Activities" pages that children do "research." Children can go to the school library, or you can provide books in your classroom that pertain to the subject the children are to "research." For nonreaders, make tapes containing the necessary information and make them available at a listening center.

Each sound of the week also has two reproducible pages that can be folded and stapled to make an eight-page chart story booklet for children to illustrate. After duplicating both pages, fold each page in half lengthwise and then fold in half the other direction.

Slip one folded page inside the other.

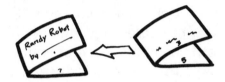

Staple the left side of the booklet. (You don't need to cut all eight pages apart to staple them in the correct order.)

The booklet ends with four words from the story that children are to illustrate. Before you give the booklet to the children, brainstorm how to illustrate these words. Adjectives or verbs may be harder to illustrate than nouns. For example, if children are to illustrate the word *fast,* they can draw a picture of *something that is fast* to show their comprehension of the word.

Follow the basic lesson guide format and be creative in adding the additional activities to meet the individual needs of your students.

Weekly Lesson Guide

Day 1

Letter/Sound Introduction
Introduce by name and sound the letter to be studied for the week. Write the letter (capital and lowercase) on the chalkboard or large chart.

Brainstorming Session
Brainstorm words that begin with the presented sound with the children. As each child gives a word, write it on the chalkboard or chart and make an illustration for it if possible. Continue adding words until the chalkboard or chart is filled. Leave this list of words up for the entire week.

Puppet
Bagging It with Puppets! (Wick and Mehrens, Fearon Teacher Aids, 1988) provides patterns for puppets that accompany each sound of the week. To introduce the puppet of the week to the children, attach a large grocery bag with a giant question mark on it to the chalkboard or a special spot. Put the puppet of the week inside the grocery bag. The child who guessed the puppet name during the brainstorming session will remove the puppet from the bag and present it to the class. After this introduction, help each child assemble a puppet according to the directions.

Day 2

Chart Story
Introduce the chart story for the letter/sound of the week (see pages 138–40). Write the story on sentence strips, a large chart, or on the chalkboard. Ask the children:
1. Who can find the word that tells . . .
2. Who can find a word that rhymes with . . .
3. Who can find a word that has three syllables?
4. Who can find a word that begins like . . .

Read the story in a variety of ways:
Use a low voice, high voice, or a loud voice.
Read the story fast or slow.
Snap your fingers and read.
Clap and read.

Day 3

Review Chart Story
Transfer the story to sentence strips before beginning the lesson. Show the children each sentence strip and have them identify each word. Cut the words apart as children read them. Give each child a word. Continue until the entire story is cut apart and each child has a word. Then rebuild the story by matching the words in the same order as they appear in the chart story, which is written on a chart or chalkboard.

Day 4

Review
Place a new set of chart story sentence strips that are not in the proper sequence on the chalkboard rail or in a chart holder. Have children put the sentence strips in the proper sequence.

Day 5

Conclusion
Review chart story. Have children read and illustrate their own copies of the chart story, which have been reproduced and stapled together in eight-page booklets (see reproducible pages that accompany each sound). Puppets and books go home today!

Teacher-Directed Classwork Activities

Choose several activities each week.

1. Write several categories on a chalkboard or chart. Have children select the words from the brainstorm list that fit the correct categories. Write the words for the children. Then allow them to come to the chalkboard or chart and add illustrations. Some category suggestions include the following: something you can hear, something you can play with, or something you can ride.

2. Say, "I am thinking of a word that rhymes with ____." Have a child come up to the brainstorm list and "frame" with his or her hands the word that rhymes.

3. Fold a sheet of 18" x 24" newsprint in half lengthwise for each child. Then fold it into fourths. Cut slits on the fold lines in the top sheet. Have children choose four words from the brainstorm list and write one word on each top section of their papers. Have the students lift the flaps and illustrate the words underneath.

4. Write four to six scrambled sentences on the chalkboard. Emphasize capitalization and punctuation by having children come to the chalkboard, unscramble the sentences, and write them in the proper sequence. Or, emphasize word order by having students put a number above each word to indicate which comes first, second, and so on, instead of rewriting the sentence.

5. Ask each child to write a sentence (or dictate it for you to write) about the puppet of the week. Combine all sentences into an accordion booklet.

6. Cut a giant letter of the week from colored construction paper. Allow students to decorate it with drawings, pictures from magazines, and words that begin with that letter.

7. Give each child an envelope with flashcards containing vocabulary from the chart story. Describe one of the words and have children hold up their flashcards with the appropriate word written on it. For example: "I'm thinking of a man who travels in space." The children would hold up their "astronaut" flashcards.

Independent Seatwork Activities

Choose several activities each week.

1. For each child, fold a 12" x 18" sheet of newsprint into eight equal sections. Let children choose eight of their favorite words from the brainstorm list. Have them write one word in each section and illustrate it.

2. Prepare a reproducible page with eight words from the brainstorm list. Ask children to cut the words apart and paste and illustrate them on the folded newsprint. Or, have children paste the words in alphabetical order.

3. Prepare a reproducible page with four sentences, using words from the brainstorm list. There should be one word from the list in each sentence. Have children cut the sentences apart and then paste and illustrate the sentences on 12" x 18" sheets of newsprint that have been folded into fourths.

4. Prepare a reproducible page with eight words from the brainstorm list that each have a letter missing. Have children complete the words, cut them apart, and paste and illustrate them on newsprint.

5. Prepare a reproducible page with four to six words from the brainstorm list or chart story. Have the children illustrate the words and then make an illustration of each word's opposite.

6. Write six unfinished sentences on the chalkboard. Children find the missing words from the brainstorm list and write the completed sentences on lined paper. Illustrations can be added.

7. Write six scrambled sentences on the board. Have the children unscramble the words and write them in the correct order on their papers, so that the sentences make sense.

8. Prepare a reproducible page, using the chart story sentences written out of sequence. Children cut out the sentences, put the story into proper order, and glue the sentences on a sheet of paper.

9. Prepare a reproducible word search with words from the brainstorm list. Put one word in each row and provide students with a list of words to search for.

had
accident
Andrea
ambulance

b	t	a	c	c	i	d	e	n	t
h	a	d	i	s	m	h	u	r	t
A	n	d	r	e	a	t	t	e	e
l	i	c	h	e	r	d	f	g	h
i	a	m	b	u	l	a	n	c	e
d	f	h	c	a	m	e	l	i	n
f	o	r	z	w	g	o	e	s	k
A	s	t	r	o	n	a	u	t	q
d	o	f	f	c	r	s	v	a	n

Independent Homework Activities

Choose several activities each week.

1. Have children bring objects and/or pictures from home that begin with the sound of the week. Place the objects on a special table or bulletin board that has been set up for this purpose.

2. Send home a headband for each child with the letter/sound of the week stapled to it. Students decorate the headbands with things beginning with that sound.

3. Send home a blank, six-page newsprint booklet (4 1/2" x 6") with each child. Students fill the booklets with pictures that begin with the sound of the week. Pictures may be drawn by the students or cut from magazines or newspapers.

4. Challenge children to make a cartoon strip about the puppet of the week.

5. Have students bring something from home pertaining to the sound of the week in a sealed sack. After giving clues, classmates must guess the contents of the bag. The winner receives a sticker!

6. Have each child find a cardboard box at home (an empty cereal box works well) and decorate it with pictures that begin with the sound of the week.
   Or, have children glue the pictures on a sheet of paper to make a collage.

7. Have children make a list of everything they can find at home that begins with the sound of the week. Family members can help spell words.

Part One: Sounds

consonants
short vowels
long vowels

Special Activities for *Rr*

Introduce the sound of the week, using the Randy Robot puppet (see *Bagging It with Puppets!*), and present the Randy Robot chart story (page 139).

Music

"Did You Ever See a Robot?" (page 141).

Language Arts

Books:
Bunting, Eve. *Robot Birthday*. New York: Dutton, 1980.

Gatland, Kenneth. *Robots: Science and Medicine into the 21st Century*. London: Usborne Publishing Ltd., 1979.

Greene, Carol. *Robots*. Chicago: Children's Press, 1983.

Krahn, Fernando. *Robot-bot-bot*. New York: Dutton, 1979.

Titus, Eve. *Anatole and the Robot*. New York: McGraw-Hill, 1960.

Poetry:
Cromwell, Liz. "Robbie the Rabbit." In *Finger Frolics,* pg. 6. Luonia, Michigan: Partner Press, 1983.

Sullivan, Joan. "Round Is a Pancake." In *Treasure Chest of Poetry,* pg. 6. Allen, Texas: DLM Teaching Resources, 1986.

Cooking

Randy Robot's Racy Raisin Ripple (page 155).

Handwriting

Silly sentence: Randy Robot's red roadster races rapidly.

Give each child a copy of Randy's *R* Words (page 13).

Math/Language

Read the poem "Round Is a Pancake" to the class. Have each student draw a picture of a round object on a round sheet of paper. Combine all pictures to make a "round" book. Try making a "rectangle" book, too!

Art

Children can make three-dimensional robots! Have each child cover a half-gallon milk carton with aluminum foil, or an adult can help spray the cartons with silver paint. Make a round hole on both sides of each carton and slip a cardboard tube (paper towel or tissue tube) through the holes for arms. Children can glue on "junk" (wood or metal scraps, jar lids, spools, cans, egg cartons, paper cups, and small boxes) they bring from home. A hot glue gun works well, but children should not use it unless supervised. This art project is best done in small groups with adult assistance.

tube

milk carton

Randy's R Words

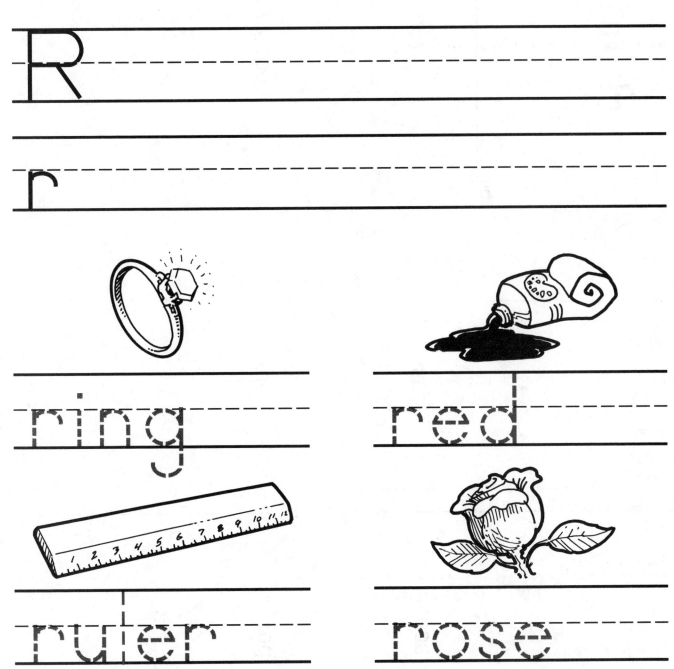

R — — — — — — — — — — — — — — — — — —

r — — — — — — — — — — — — — — — — — —

ring   red

ruler   rose

Randy Robot

by _____

See Randy Robot.

2

1

Words from Our Story

run

7

red

8

fast

racer

See Randy's racer go fast!

6

Go Randy! Go! Go! Go!

5

See Randy Robot run.

3

See Randy Robot run to the red racer.

4

Special Activities for *Ss*

> Introduce the sound of the week, using the Silly Scarecrow puppet (see *Bagging It with Puppets!*), and present the Silly Scarecrow chart story (page 139).

Music

"Silly Scarecrow" (page 141).

Language Arts

Books:

Farber, Norma. *There Goes Feathertop!* New York: Unicorn-Dutton, 1979.

Gordon, Sharon. *Sam the Scarecrow.* Mahwah, NJ: Troll Association, 1980.

Hart, Jeanne. *Scareboy.* Orleans, MA: Parnassus, 1957.

Oana, Kay D. *Robbie and the Raggedy Scarecrow.* Fayetteville, GA: Oddo, 1978.

Tripp, Paul. *The Strawman Who Smiled by Mistake.* New York: Doubleday, 1967.

Poetry:

Bacmesiter, Rhoda. "Galoshes." In *A New Treasury of Children's Poetry,* pg. 28. New York: Doubleday, 1984.

Scott, Louise B., and, Lucille F. Wood. "I'll Make a Scarecrow." In *Singing Fun,* pg. 1. St. Louis: Webster Publishing Co., 1954.

———."The Scarecrow." In *Singing Fun,* pg. 4. St. Louis: Webster Publishing Co., 1954.

Cooking

Silly Scarecrow's Scrumptious Skillet Spaghetti (page 156).

Handwriting

Silly sentence: Silly Scarecrow scribbles silly stories.

Give children a copy of Silly's *S* Words (page 17).

Science/Art

Plant seeds in planters and place them in a sunny spot in the classroom. (This project is best when done in the spring.) Children can use white construction paper and permanent black markers to draw silly scarecrows. Have children decorate the scarecrows, using paint or crayons, and then cut them out. Staple or glue the scarecrows on tongue depressors and place them in the planters to scare the birds away! (Be sure the scarecrows are not blocking the sun.)

Math

Have children bring a variety of seeds to school. Classify the seeds by color, size, and shape. Then allow children to plant the seeds and make graphs to record growth results.

Silly's S Words

S

s

sun

snake

snow

six

Silly Scarecrow

by _____

Can you see Silly Scarecrow?

2

1

funny

pants

Words from Our Story

7   jacket

8   hat

Silly Scarecrow looks funny.

3

See its funny pants.

6

See its funny hat.

4

See its funny jacket.

5

Special Activities for *Tt*

> Introduce the sound of the week, using the Tanya Tiger puppet (see *Bagging It with Puppets!*), and present the Tanya Tiger chart story (page 140).

Music

"Tanya Tiger" (page 142).

Language Arts

Books:
Seuss, Dr. *I Can Lick 30 Tigers Today.* New York: Random House, 1969.

Sharmot, Marjorie Weinman. *I'm Terrific.* New York: Holiday House, 1977.

Supraner, Robyn. *Would You Rather Be a Tiger?* Boston: Houghton Mifflin, 1973.

Tworkov, Jack. *Tigers Don't Bite.* New York: Dutton, 1956.

Whitney, Alex. *Once a Bright Red Tiger.* New York: Walck, 1973.

Poetry:
Foster, John. "Tiger." In *A Very First Poetry Book,* pg. 86. New York: Oxford University Press, 1984.

Prelutsky, Jack. "The Bengal Tiger." In *Zoo Doings,* pg. 18. New York: Greenwillow, 1983.

Cooking

Tanya Tiger's Terrific Twists (page 156).

Handwriting

Silly sentence: Tanya Tiger tickles Terry Turtle's toes.

Give each child a copy of Tanya's *T* Words (page 21).

Math

Go on a tiger hunt! Make orange construction-paper tiger tails with math problems written on them. Give a tail to each child. If the children can solve the problems in a predetermined amount of time, they can put the tails on their tigers, which are in the tiger cages (see art project below).

Science

Children can make a terrarium by filling the bottom of an aquarium with potting soil, planting a variety of houseplants in the soil, watering them, and covering the top of the aquarium with plastic wrap.

Art

Give each child a shoe box, yarn, and colored construction paper to make a pet tiger in a cage. Children can add their tiger tails from the math activity.

Tanya's T Words

T

t

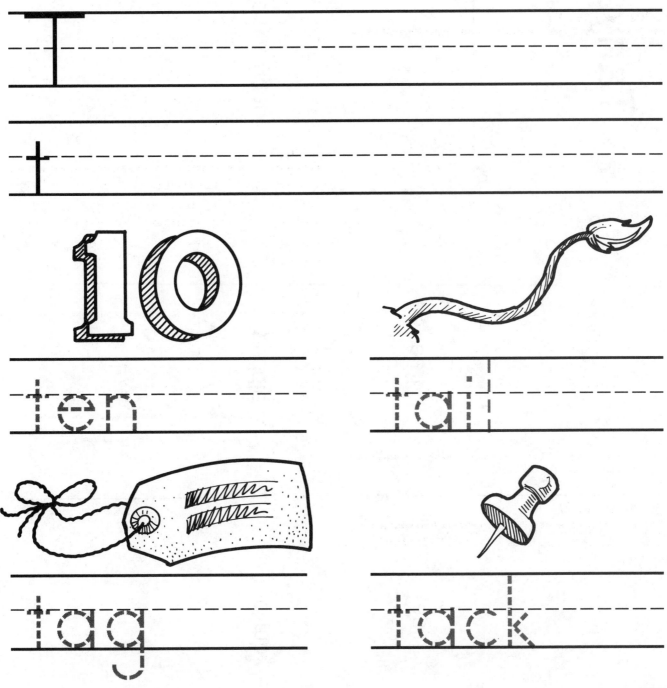

10

ten

tail

tag

tack

Tanya Tiger

by _____

"Rr-r-r-r!" said Tanya Tiger.

2

1

Words from Our Story

puddle   climb

7

tree

8

hide

"I can hide in a bush."

6

5

"I can climb a tree."

"I can jump over a puddle."

3

4

"I can run in the grass."

Special Activities for *Mm*

Introduce the sound of the week, using the Merry Mouse puppet (see *Bagging It with Puppets!*), and present the Merry Mouse chart story (page 139).

Music

"Merry Mouse" (page 142).

Language Arts

Books:
Carle, Eric. *Do You Want to Be My Friend?* New York: Crowell, 1971.
De Paola, Tomie. *Charlie Needs a Cloak.* Englewood Cliffs, NJ: Prentice-Hall, 1973.
Hewett, Joan. *The Mouse and the Elephant.* Boston: Little, 1977.
Lionni, Leo. *Frederick.* New York: Pantheon, 1967.
Titus, Eve. *Anatole.* New York: McGraw-Hill, 1957.

Poetry:
Allen, Marie Louise. "The Mitten Song." In *Treasure Chest of Poetry*, pg. 63. Allen, Texas: DLM Teaching Resources, 1986.
Fyleman, Rose, "Mice." In *Treasure Chest of Poetry*, pg. 77. Allen, Texas: DLM Teaching Resources, 1986.
Lee, Dennis. "The Muddy Puddle." In *Treasure Chest of Poetry*, pg. 152. Allen, Texas: DLM Teaching Resources, 1986.
Mitchell, Lucy. "The House of the Mouse." In *A New Treasury of Children's Poetry*, pg. 24. New York: Doubleday, 1984.
Mullins, Edward. In *Animal Limericks*, pgs. 14–15. Chicago: Follett, 1966.

Cooking

Merry Mouse's Marvelous Muffins (page 153).

Handwriting

Silly sentence: Merry Mouse munches marshmallows.

Give each child a copy of Merry's *M* Words (page 25).

Art/Math

Prepare a pair of construction-paper mittens for each child by cutting out four mitten patterns and stapling each pair together around the edges. The mittens should be large enough for the child's hands to fit through the bottom opening. Discuss design, pattern, and symmetry. Find objects in the classroom with symmetry. (Their own mittens are an excellent example!) Then let children create designs on their mittens with construction paper, sponge painting, or sewing notions (ribbon, lace, rickrack).

When mittens are complete, attach a long piece of yarn to each pair to keep them together. Sing "The Mitten Song" while children sway their mittened hands back and forth.

Merry's **M** Words

M
_____

m
_____

mouse

mask

mittens

milk

Merry Mouse

"M-m-m-m-m!" said Merry Mouse.

2

1

by _____

mess

make

7

8

merry

mud

"I will make a merry, merry mess!"

"I will make some mud pies."

6

3

5

4

"I will make a mess!"

"I will make many, many mud pies."

Special Activities for *Ff*

> Introduce the sound of the week, using the Firefighter Fred or Firefighter Frances puppet (see *Bagging It with Puppets!*), and present the Firefighter Fred chart story (page 138).

Music

"Did You Ever Meet a Firefighter?" (page 142).

Language Arts

Books:

Cole, L. D. *Sparky Fireman*. Chicago: Follett, 1968.

Collier, James Lincoln. *Visit to the Firehouse*. Chicago, Illinois: Benefic Press, 1966.

Meshover, Leonard. *You Visit a Fire Station*. Chicago, Illinois: Benefic Press, 1965.

Slobodkin, Louis. *Read about Fireman*. New York: Vanguard Press, 1967.

Zaffo, George J. *The Big Book of Real Fire Engines*. New York: Doubleday,1950.

Poetry:

Firefighters

Five little firefighters, standing in
   a row.
The firebell sounds and they all
   have to go!
The engine it roars, it jangles
   and clangs,
Fast down the street with noises
   and bangs.
They put out the fire with water
   and foam,
Then pack up their hoses and go
   slowly home.

Cooking

Firefighter Fred's Fantastic Fudgesicles (page 150).

Handwriting

Silly sentence: Firefighter Fred fights fires frantically.
   Give each child a copy of Fred's *F* Words (page 29).

Science/Math

Find and count as many objects in the classroom that begin with *F* as you can. Include names of children and body parts. Graph the results.

   Make fog in a bottle! You will need a juice bottle, one cup of hot water, and an ice cube. Put the hot water in the bottle and set an ice cube on top of the bottle opening. The fog will form inside the bottle.

   Make a book of various animal and fowl footprint pictures. Mount the pictures on tagboard with a pocket at the bottom of each. Children can refer to library books to identify the prints, and then place name cards in the pockets. Provide a chart showing the name of each footprint, so children can check to see if they are correct.

Art

Children can finger-paint, make footprints by using various types of shoes, or make a collage of funny faces.

Something Special

Visit a neighborhood fire station, or arrange for a firefighter to visit the classroom.

F

Fred's F Words

F
F

f
f

fan

five

foot

fork

Firefighter Fred

by _____

Here is Firefighter Fred.

2

1

truck

dog

7

fight

Fire!

8

Here go Fred and Fritz to fight the fire.

Here is Fred's dog, Fritz.

6

3

5

4

Er-r-r-r! Fire! Fire! Fire!

Here is Fred's fire truck.

Special Activities for *Bb*

> Introduce the sound of the week, using the Billy Boy puppet (see *Bagging It with Puppets!*), and present the Billy Boy chart story (page 138).

Music

"Billy Boy, Billy Boy" or "B-I-L-L-Y" (page 142).

Language Arts

Books:

Christian, Mary Blount. *The Sand Lot.* New York: Harvey House, 1978.

Hillert, Margaret. *Play Ball.* Chicago: Follett, 1978.

Hoff, Syd. *Slugger Sal's Slump.* New York: Dutton, 1979.

———. *The Littlest Leaguer.* New York: Dutton, 1976.

Sharp, Paul. *Paul the Pitcher.* Chicago: Children's Press, 1984.

Poetry:

Foster, John. "Billy's Bath." In *A Very First Poetry Book,* pg. 32. New York: Oxford University Press, 1979.

Ireson, Barbara. "The Lost Ball." In *The Barnes Book of Nursery Verse,* pg. 8. San Diego, CA: A. S. Barnes, 1960.

Silverstein, Shel. "Play Ball." In *A Light in the Attic,* pg. 131. New York: Harper & Row, 1981.

Cooking

Billy Boy's Best Burgers (page 148).

Handwriting

Silly sentence: Billy Boy bats big blue balls.

Give each child a copy of Billy's *B* Words (page 33).

Science/Math

Discuss bubbles. Mix 1 teaspoon powdered detergent with 1/3 cup water to make a bubble solution. Give each child a small amount of the solution in a paper cup. Allow children to blow bubbles, using drinking straws. (This activity is best done outdoors. Be sure children do not ingest the bubble solution.)

See how far each child can roll a ball or how long the ball can be kept bouncing. Then make a chart or graph to display the results.

Discuss *big, bigger,* and *biggest.*

Play a beanbag game.

Art

Children can make baseball mobiles. Have each child draw and cut a bat from a 7" x 4" piece of brown construction paper (or have a pattern available to trace), a mitt from an 8" x 8" piece of brown construction paper, and Billy's face from an 8" x 6" piece of skin-tone construction paper. Children may want to make baseball caps also. Make a construction-paper tube for each child by rolling a 12" x 18" piece of construction paper. Have children hang their objects from the tubes with string.

Something Special

Children can "research" information about balls. Then make a ball-shaped book and glue pictures of different kinds of balls inside. Use catalogs and magazines for ideas and pictures.

Billy's B Words

B ------

b ------

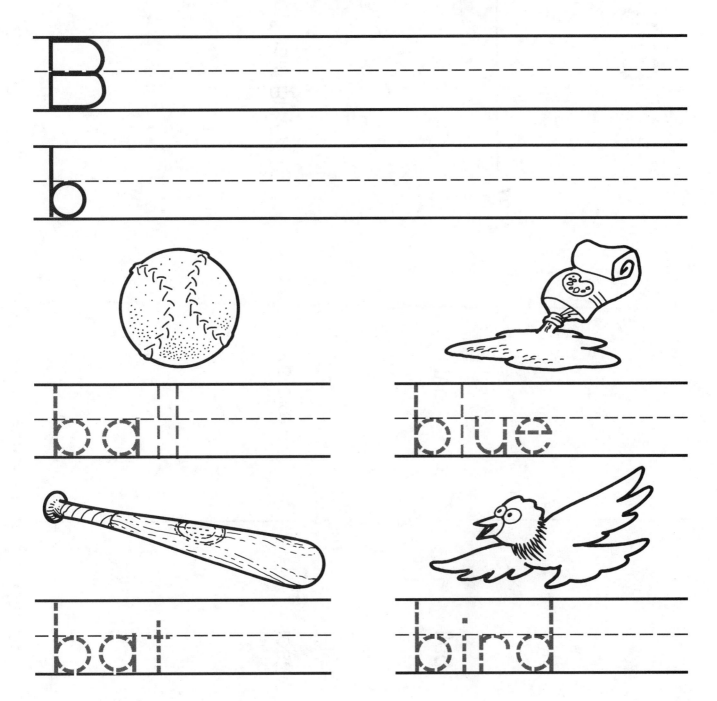

ball

blue

bat

bird

Billy Boy

"Boo-hoo-hoo," said Billy.

2

1

bɑ

broke

7

lost

bɑt

8

ball

bɑ

"I lost the ball! Boo-hoo-hoo!"

6

"I broke the bat."

"I had a new bat."

3

"I had a new ball."

4

Special Activities for *Cc*

> Introduce the sound of the week, using the Cowboy Curly or Cowgirl Chris puppet (see *Bagging It with Puppets!*), and present the Cowboy Curly chart story (page 138).

Music

"Cowboy Curly" (page 142).

Language Arts

Books:

Greene, Carla. *Cowboys: What Do They Do?* New York: Harper & Row, 1972.

Hillert, Margaret. *The Little Cowboy and the Big Cowboy.* Chicago: Follett, 1980.

Krasilovsky, Phyllis. *The Girl Who Was a Cowboy.* New York: Doubleday, 1956.

Lenski, Lois. *Cowboy Small.* New York: Oxford University Press, 1949.

Slobodkin, Florence. *Cowboy Twins.* New York: Vanguard Press, 1960.

Poetry:

Curly

Out on the prairie Curly will ride,
Rounding up steers that will all try to hide.
Lasso in hand, it twirls with a hiss,
He also gets help from a cowgirl named Chris.
He sleeps in a tent when nighttime is here,
And listens to the noises of coyote and deer.
In the morning a chuckwagon puts food in his hand,
Then Curly is off, for there's cattle to brand.

Cooking

Cowboy Curly's Crunchy Candy (page 149).

Handwriting

Silly sentence: Cowboy Curly catches coral-colored cows.

Give each child a copy of Curly's *C* Words (page 37).

Math

Tell children that they will be drawing five cowboys or cowgirls. Then, to give children practice recognizing ordinal numbers, have the following directions written on the chalkboard for them to follow or give the directions orally:

Draw the 4th one tall and thin.
Draw the 2nd one fat and short.
Draw the 5th one whirling a rope.
Draw the 3rd one riding a horse.
Draw the 1st one playing a guitar.

Art

Each child can make a stick horse by stuffing a paper lunch sack with newspaper. Tie the sacks shut for children with masking tape. Children can glue on ears, nose, tongue, and a mane created from construction paper. Use masking tape or a stapler to attach the bags to sticks made from rolled butcher paper. Play some galloping music and children can ride off into the sunset!

Something Special

Have a cowboy-style cookout.

Curly's C Words

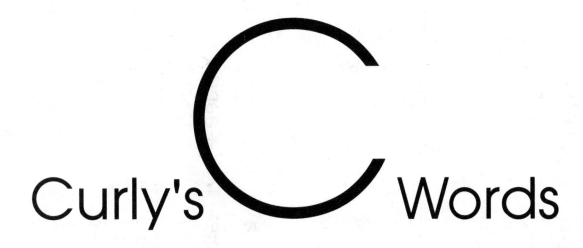

C

c

cat

cow

car

cap

Cowboy Curly

by _____

"Yippee-i-yay!" said Cowboy Curly.

2

1

Words from Our Story

horse   ride

7

guitar   fire

8

"I play my guitar."

6

"I sit by the fire."

5

"I can ride a horse."

3

"I can rope a calf."

4

Special Activities for *Dd*

Introduce the sound of the week, using the Doctor Donna or Doctor Dan puppets (see *Bagging It with Puppets!*), and present the Doctor Donna chart story (page 138).

Music

"Doctor Donna" (page 143).

Language Arts

Books:

Berenstain, Stan. *The Berenstain Bears Go to the Doctor.* New York: Random House, 1981.

Charlip, Remy. *Mother, Mother I Feel Sick.* New York: Parents, 1966.

Greene, Carla. *Doctors and Nurses: What Do They Do?* New York: Harper & Row, 1963.

Robison, Deborah. *Your Turn, Doctor.* New York: Dial Press, 1982.

Rockwell, Harlow. *My Doctor.* New York: Macmillan, 1973.

Poetry:

Lee, Dennis. "Doctor, Doctor." In *Jelly Belly,* pg. 37. London: Blantyre Printing & Binding Ltd., 1983.

Nicholls, Judith. "The Dentist." In *Another First Poetry Book,* pg. 47. New York: Oxford University Press, 1987.

Silverstein, Shel. "Examination." In *A Light in the Attic.* New York: Harper & Row, 1981.

Cooking

Doctor Dan's Divine Peanut Butter Play Dough (page 149).

Handwriting

Silly sentence: Doctor Donna dunks delicious donuts.

Give children a copy of Dan's *D* Words (page 41).

Art

Dandy Dough

In a mixing bowl, mix:
    2 cups flour
    2 cups salt
    1/2 cup (or more) hot water
    1 tablespoon powdered alum
    1 teaspoon cooking oil
Add food coloring if desired. Children can make flat or three-dimensional objects on waxed paper. Let the dough objects dry for several days or bake them for about 3 hours at 245° F. Children can then paint the objects with dots and shellac them.

Math

Teach children how to play dominoes.

Something Special

Visit a doctor's office or hospital. Invite a doctor or dentist to visit the classroom.

Set up a doctor's office or medical center in the classroom.

Discuss health, safety, and good nutrition.

Dan's D Words

D

d

desk

door

dime

doll

Doctor Donna

by _____

See Doctor Donna.

2

1

Words from Our Story

dizzy Help!

7

doctor nurse

8

Help dizzy Dot!

6

Help! Doctor Donna!

5

See her nurse, Dot.

3

4

Dot is dizzy.

Special Activities for *Gg*

> Introduce the sound of the week, using the Greta Girl puppet (see *Bagging It with Puppets!*), and present the Greta Girl chart story (page 138).

Music

"Greta Girl" (page 143).

Language Arts

Books:

Carle, Eric. *The Grouchy Ladybug.* New York: Crowell, 1977.

Klein, Norma. *Girls Can Be Anything.* New York: Dutton, 1973.

Sharmat, Marjorie Weinman. *Grumley the Grouch.* New York: Holiday House, 1980.

Spier, Peter. *Gobble, Growl, Grunt.* New York: Doubleday, 1971.

Poetry:

Greta

Greta lost her green galoshes,
She also lost her golden gown.
She didn't lose her gooey gumdrops,
So she won't wear a frown!

Cooking

Greta Girl's Granola (page 151).

Handwriting

Silly sentence: Greta Girl grows green grasshoppers.

Give each child a copy of Greta's *G* Words (page 45).

Science/Math

Give each child an 8 1/2" x 3 1/2" strip of skin-tone construction paper. Have children draw Greta's face in the middle of the paper and glue construction-paper strips on both sides of the face for hair. Children can curl the hair strips around a pencil before gluing them in place. Then glue the face strips around soup cans. Children fill the cans with potting soil, sprinkle grass seed on top, and water. They can watch Greta's "hair" grow. Measure daily and keep a record of the growth. Give Greta a "haircut" and watch to see how many days it takes for the "hair" to grow back.

Art

Children can make Greta's gift boxes by covering boxes with cloth and decorating them with discarded jewelry and sequins. The boxes can be given as gifts on Mother's Day, birthdays, or other special occasions.

Greta's G Words

G

g

ghost   gum

grass   goat

Greta Girl

by _____

"Grumble, grumble, grumble, grumble," groans Greta.

2

1

galoshes

gumdrops

glove

gooey

7

8

"But I can find my gooey gumdrops!"

6

"I can't find my gold gown."

5

"I can't find my green galoshes."

3

"I can't find my gray glove."

4

Special Activities for *Hh*

> Introduce the sound of the week, using the Harry Hippopotamus puppet (see *Bagging It with Puppets!*), and present the Harry Hippopotamus chart story (page 138).

Music

"Harry Hippo" (page 143).

Language Arts

Books:

Moore, Nancy. *The Unhappy Hippopotamus.* New York: Vanguard Press, 1957.

Standon, Anna. *Hippo Had Hiccups.* New York: Coward-McCann, 1964.

Waber, Bernard. *You Look Ridiculous.* Boston: Houghton Mifflin, 1966.

Croswell, Volney. *How to Hide a Hippopotamus.* New York: Dodd, Mead & Co., 1958.

Thaler, Mike. *There's a Hippopotamus Under My Bed.* New York: Watts, 1977.

Poetry:

Cole, William. "The Hippo." In *Pick Me Up,* pg. 86. New York: Macmillan, 1972.

John Foster "Hippopotamus." In *A Very First Poetry Book,* pg. 82. New York: Oxford University Press, 1982.

————. "Though Hippos Weigh at Least a Ton." In *A Very First Poetry Book,* pg. 83. New York: Oxford University Press, 1982.

Gardner, John. "The Hippopotamus." In *A Child's Bestiary,* pg. 29. New York: Alfred A. Knopf, 1977.

Prelutsky, Jack. "The Hippopotamus." In *Zoo Doings,* pg. 56. New York: Greenwillow Books, 1983.

Cooking

Harry Hippo's Happy Hot Dogs (page 151).

Handwriting

Silly sentence: Harry Hippopotamus hops home happily.

Give each child a copy of Harry's *H* Words (page 49).

Science/Math

Have hopping relays and chart the results.

Children can "research" to make a list of things that hop and then use the list to make a hopping book.

Art

Give each child a ball of clay the size of a softball. Have children use their fists to punch a hole in the center of the clay ball. Next, they pinch out four legs, a head, and ears to make a happy hippo. Children can use water to moisten fingers and smooth out the sculpture. (Don't expect perfection! Give assistance to children only when needed.) Fire in kiln. Children can then add details with paint and yarn for a tail.

Something Special

Have a "Hot Dog Day."

Harry's H Words

H

h

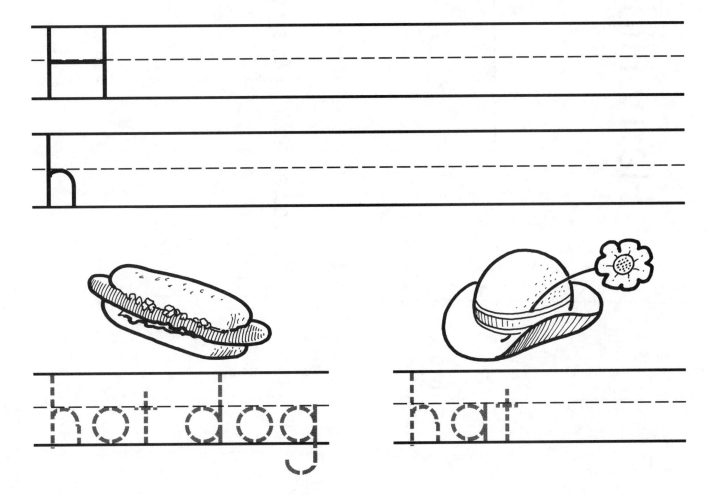

hot dog

hat

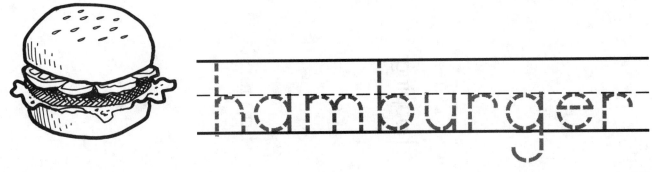

hamburger

It's All in the Bag! © 1990 Fearon Teacher Aids

49

Harry Hippopotamus

by _____

Hop! Hop! Hop! goes Harry Hippopotamus.

2

1

one

two

hot dog

7

8

hopping

Hot dogs for you!

First on one foot.

6

3

5

4

Hopping to the hippo market.

Then on two.

Special Activities for *Jj*

> Introduce the sound of the week, using the Jack-in-the-Box puppet (see *Bagging It with Puppets!*), and present the Jack-in-the-Box chart story (page 139).

Music

"Jack is Jumping Up and Down" (page 143).

Language Arts

Books:
Enderle, Judith A. *Good Junk*. New York: Elsevier/Nelson Books, 1981.

Mahari, Jabari. *The Day They Stole the Letter J*. Third World Press, 1981.

Miller, Edna. *Jumping Bean*. Englewood Cliffs, NJ: Prentice-Hall, 1980.

Shaw, Nancy. *Sheep in a Jeep*. New York: Houghton Mifflin, 1986.

Young, Miriam Burt. *Jellybeans for Breakfast*. New York: Parents, 1968.

Poetry:
Jack-in-the-Box sits so still.
(Children curl up.)
Will you come out?
Yes, I will.
(Children pop up, but their feet must not leave the ground or they are a "broken" jack-in-the-box.)

Cooking

Jack-in-the-Box Juicesicles (page 152).

Handwriting

Silly sentence: Jack-in-the-Box jumps joyfully.

Give children a copy of Jack's *J* Words (page 53).

Science/Math

Measure how far each child can jump on one foot, two feet, backward, or sideways.

Bring in some Mexican jumping beans. Find out what makes them jump. Have a bean-jumping contest.

Art

J is for jewelry and junk! Children can make junk jewelry necklaces.

Something Special

Have a junk exchange or swap.

Have a "joke" day or make a class joke book.

Jack's J Words

J

j

jar

jump

jewel

junk

Jack-in-the-Box

by _____

Jump! Jump! Jump! goes Jack.

2

1

Words from Our Story

jump

7 _____

up and down

clown

8

go

Back down you go.

6

5

Oh! Oh! Oh!

Up and down, up and down.

3

4

Like a very happy clown.

Special Activities for *Ll*

> Introduce the sound of the week, using the Lionel Lion puppet (see *Bagging It with Puppets!*), and present the Lionel Lion chart story (page 139).

Music

"Lionel the Lion" (page 143).

Language Arts

Books:
Daugherty, James. *Andy and the Lion.* New York: Viking, 1938.

Fatio, Louise. *The Happy Lion.* New York: McGraw-Hill, 1954.

Freeman, Don. *Dandelion.* New York: Viking, 1964.

Hurd, Edith. *Johnny Lion's Bad Day.* New York: Harper & Row, 1970.

Varga, Judy. *Miss Lollipop's Lion.* New York: Morrow, 1963.

Poetry:
Prelutsky, Jack. "The Lion." In *The Random House Book of Poetry for Children,* pg. 61. New York: Random House, 1983.

Aldis, Dorothy. "Lovely Lion." In *Here, There and Everywhere,* pg. 23. New York: Minton, Balch & Co., 1936.

Marantz, Vic. "Leo, the Lion." In *Growing with Music.* Englewood Cliffs, NJ: Prentice-Hall, 1970.

Cooking

Lionel Lion's Luscious Lemonade (page 153).

Handwriting

Silly sentence: Lionel Lion loves lemon lollipops.

Give each child a copy of Lionel's *L* Words (page 57).

Bulletin Board Idea

Make a lollipop tree! Make a large, bare tree on a bulletin board or large piece of butcher paper. Each child makes an *L* picture on one side of a cardboard lollipop and decorates the other side with yarn, rickrack, felt, ribbon, or crayons. Attach lollipops to tongue depressors and display them on the lollipop tree.

Art

Children can make ladybug pet rocks! Go for a walk around the neighborhood to collect rocks. Or, have children bring flat, round rocks from home. Children paint the top of the rocks with red paint. When the red paint dries, black spots can be added. Cover with shellac and add legs and antennae, using black pipe cleaners secured with a hot glue gun. (Children should not use the hot glue gun without supervision.)

Something Special

Have each student write a story about his or her pet ladybug or make a class book about ladybugs.

Lionel's L Words

L

lion

lemon

ladybug

lollipop

Lionel Lion

by _____

Lionel Lion loves lollipops.

2

1

round

big

7

8

lollipops

little

Yum! Yum! Yum!

6

Lemon ones, too!

5

Big ones, little ones, round ones, too.

3

Red ones, green ones,

4

Special Activities for *Nn*

Introduce the sound of the week, using the Nurse Nancy or Nurse Ned puppet (see *Bagging It with Puppets!*), and present the Nurse Nancy chart story (page 139).

Music

"N-A-N-C-Y" (page 144).

Language Arts

Books:

Arnold, Caroline. *Who Keeps Us Healthy?* New York: Watts, 1982.

Gaeddert, Lou Ann Bigge. *Noisy Nancy Nora.* New York: Doubleday, 1965.

Kraus, Robert. *Rebecca Hatpin.* New York: E. P. Dutton, 1974.

Leaf, Munro. *Noodle.* New York: Four Winds Press, 1965.

Whitney, Alma Marshak. *Just Awful.* Reading, MA: Addison-Wesley, 1971.

Poetry:

Blake, William. "Nurse's Song." In *From Morn to Midnight.* New York: Crowell, 1977.

Hymes, Lucia, and James Hymes, Jr. "Oodles of Noodles." In *The Random House Book of Poetry for Children,* pg. 147. New York: Random House, 1983.

Liu, Shu Ning. "My Nurse." In *I Sing the Song of Myself,* pg. 13. New York: Greenwillow, 1978.

Cooking

Nancy Nurse's Nifty Nachos (page 154).

Handwriting

Silly sentence: Nancy Nurse nibbles nachos.

Give each child a copy of Nancy's *N* Words (page 61).

Math

Make a classroom "nine" book. Each child can make one page with nine *N* objects.

Art

Provide dyed macaroni and string for children to make noodle necklaces. To dye the macaroni, put 5 tablespoons of vinegar and a few drops of food coloring in a glass jar. Add a handful of macaroni and put a lid on the jar. Shake the jar until macaroni is completely colored. Then lay macaroni on waxed paper to dry. Colored construction-paper flowers with holes in the middle can also be strung to make unique necklaces.

Something Special

After a visit from the school nurse, write a chart story about what the children learned.

Write a newspaper with the children.

Write stories about the week's *N* activities and send them home with the children at the end of the unit.

Nancy's N Words

N

n

nest

noodles

nail

nine

Nurse Nancy

by _____

2

1

Nurse Nancy eats nachos.

morning

night

7

8

noon

nachos

Morning, noon, and night.

Nurse Nancy eats nuts.

6

3

Nurse Nancy eats nectarines.

Nurse Nancy eats noodles.

5

4

Special Activities for *Kk*

> Introduce the sound of the week, using the Kooky Kookaburra puppet (see *Bagging It with Puppets!*), and present the Kooky Kookaburra chart story (page 139).

Music

"All the Kookaburras" (page 144).

Language Arts

Books:
Braun, Kathy. *Kangaroo and Kangaroo.* New York: Doubleday, 1965.

Kinney, Harrison. *Kangaroo in the Attic.* New York: McGraw-Hill, 1960.

Galbraith, Katharine. *Katie Did.* New York: Atheneum, 1982.

Payne, Emmy. *Katy No Pocket.* Boston: Houghton Mifflin, 1944.

Peet, Bill. *Kermit the Hermit.* Boston: Houghton Mifflin, 1965.

Poetry:

Kookaburra
Kookaburra sits in the old gum tree,
Merry, merry King of the bush is he.
Laugh, Kookaburra, laugh, Kooka-
  burra,
Gay your life must be.

Kookaburra sits in the old gum tree,
Eating all the gumdrops he can see.
Stop, Kookaburra, stop, Kookaburra,
Leave some there for me.
(Australian Round)

Cooking

Kooky's Kohlrabi Dip (page 153).

Handwriting

Silly sentence: Kooky Kookaburra kicks kettles.

Give each child a copy of Kooky's *K* Words (page 65).

Science

Discuss kites and allow children to do some "research." Encourage children to find out how kites can be useful, if some kites fly higher than others, and what conditions are necessary for kites to fly.

Math

Give each child a 30" and 36" dowel notched on both ends to make a kite. Have children measure dowels with rulers. Have them measure down eight inches on the longer dowel and make a pencil mark. Glue the 30" dowel crosswise at this mark. Give each child a piece of string that is long enough to go around the outside tips of the dowels. Children can attach string through each notch on the dowel ends. Have children lay this completed frame down on newsprint and draw a line around the frame, allowing a 2" border. Cut out the newsprint, fold the edges over the string, and glue in place.

Art

Children can decorate paper to be used for kites, using permanent markers. (Design the paper before making the kite frames.)

Kooky's K Words

K

k

kettle

kick

king

kite

Kooky Kookaburra

by

_____

Kooky Kookaburra goes to kindergarten.

2

1

teacher

7

kites

8

flies

recess

At recess, Kooky flies kites.

6

Klip-klop, klip-klop.

Mrs. King is the teacher.

3

Kooky keeps time to the music.

4

Special Activities for *Pp*

> Introduce the sound of the week, using the Peter Pig puppet (see *Bagging It with Puppets!*), and present the Peter Pig chart story on page 139.

Music

"Popping Popcorn" and "Did You Ever Eat a Pizza?" (page 144).

Language Arts

Books:
Augarde, Steve. *Pig*. New York: Bradbury Press, 1977.

De Paola, Tomie. *The Popcorn Book*. New York: Holiday House, 1978.

Goodall, John S. *The Adventures of Paddy Pork*. San Diego, CA: Harcourt Brace Jovanovich, 1968.

Lobel, Arnold. *Small Pig*. New York: Harper & Row, 1969.

The Three Little Pigs. Illus. by Paul Galdone. New York: Seabury Press, 1970.

Poetry:
Blegvad, Lenore. *This Little Pig-a-Wig and Other Rhymes about Pigs*. New York: Atheneum, 1978.

Cromwell, Liz. "Pop! Pop! Pop!" In *Finger Frolics*, pg. 106. Luonia, Michigan: Partner Press, 1983.

McGinley, Phyllis. "P's the Proud Policeman." In *Time for Poetry*, pg. 11. Chicago: Scott Foresman, 1961.

Cooking

Peter Pig's Purple Punch (page 155).

Handwriting

Silly sentence: Peter Pig paints pretty pictures.

Give each child a copy of Peter's *P* Words (page 69).

Music/Art

Teach the song "Popcorn Popping on the Apricot Tree" (*Sing with Me*, Deseret Books, 1980) to students. Each child can make a popcorn tree by drawing a bare tree on construction paper with crayons, markers, or paint and then gluing on popcorn to represent blossoms. Students can add grass and flowers to finish the picture. Remember to pop enough popcorn to eat too!

Math

Pop a batch of popcorn. Children estimate how many kernels have popped and write the estimate on a piece of paper. Count the popcorn and place each group of ten in a counting cup.

Something Special

Have a pizza party! Make pizzas in your room or school kitchen. Better yet, visit your local pizza restaurant and have the children tour the premises.

Have a "Pink and Purple Day!" Children can wear only pink or purple clothing to school on that day.

Peter's P Words

P

p

pot

pear

pizza

pig

Peter Pig

by _____

Peter Pig pops popcorn.

2

1

piles

purple

7

pink

pop

8

Popcorn popping. Pop! Pop! Pop!

6

Piles and piles of popcorn.

3

Pop! Pop! Pop!

5

Pink and purple and puffy.

4

Special Activities for *Qq*

> Introduce the sound of the week, using the Queenie Queen puppet (see *Bagging It with Puppets!*), and present the Queenie Queen chart story (page 139).

Music

"Queenie Queen" (page 144).

Language Arts

Books:
Bowden, Joan Chase. *A Hat for the Queen*. New York: Golden Press, 1974.

Mayer, Mercer. *The Queen Always Wanted to Dance*. Englewood Cliffs, NJ: Simon and Schuster, 1971.

Oxenbury, Helen. *The Queen and Rosie*. New York: Randall, Butterfield-Campbell, 1979.

Van Woerkom, Dorothy. *The Queen Who Couldn't Bake Gingerbread*. New York: Knopf, 1975.

Poetry:
Ireson, Barbara. "Queen Queen Caroline." In *The Barnes Book of Nursery Verse*, pg. 260. San Diego, CA: A. S. Barnes & Co., Inc., 1960.
———. "Queen of Hearts." In *The Barnes Book of Nursery Verse*, pg. 263. San Diego, CA: A. S. Barnes & Co., Inc., 1960.

Cooking

Queenie Queen's Quick Quencher (page 155).

Handwriting

Silly sentence: Queenie Queen's quarterback quit.

Give each child a copy of Queenie's *Q* Words (page 73).

Math

Ask a child or a team of children a math question (or a question from any other area of study), and if the question is answered correctly, an *X* or *O* can be placed on the tic-tac-toe grid.

Art

Each child can design a quilt square, using permanent colored markers on a piece of fabric. Have a parent volunteer sew the squares together. Donate the quilt to a local nursing home.

Queenie's Q Words

Q

q

quilt

question

quiet

quarter

Queenie Queen

by _____

Queenie Queen likes to quilt.

2

1

Queenie Queen

Words from Our Story

_____

quarter   7   queen

quilt   8   poor

Maybe she should quit!

6

Poor Queenie.

5

She quilts quickly and quietly.

3

She gets a quarter per quilt.

4

Special Activities for *Vv*

Introduce the sound of the week, using the Victor Viking puppet (see *Bagging It with Puppets!*), and present the Victor Viking chart story (page 140).

Music

"Victor Viking" (page 144).

Language Arts

Books:
Clarke, Helen. *Vikings.* New York: Gloucester, 1979.

D'Aulaire, Ingri. *Leif the Lucky.* New York: Doubleday, 1941.

D'Aulaire, Ingri. *Norse Gods and Giants.* New York: Doubleday, 1967.

Haugaard, Erik Christian. *Leif the Unlucky.* Boston: Houghton Mifflin, 1982.

Poetry:
Victor the Viking a puppet most
  brave,
With horns on his hat and a
  hatchet to wave.
He'll sail 'cross the sea on an ad-
  venture so bold,
Looking for diamonds, silver, and
  gold.

Cooking

Victor's Vegetable Soup (page 158).

Handwriting

Silly sentence: Victor Viking vacuums vans.

Give each child a copy of Victor's *V* Words (page 77).

Math

Fill a cloth bag with costume jewelry. Attach a worksheet to each piece of jewelry inside the bag. If a child is able to answer each problem on the worksheet correctly in a predetermined amount of time, he or she may keep the jewel for the day.

Science

Grow a window vegetable garden from the tops of the vegetables that are used to make Victor's vegetable soup. Place the vegetable tops in a shallow tray of water.

Art

Have each child bring an empty, thoroughly washed gallon bleach bottle to school to make a Viking hat. Cut the tops off the bottles and cut horns from the remaining part of the bottles. Each child glues two horns on the bottle top. When the horns are firmly attached, children spray the helmets with gold spray paint. (Put the helmet inside a cardboard box while it is being sprayed. Only do the spraying in a well-ventilated area.)

Make vegetable prints, using carrots, cabbage, or potatoes.

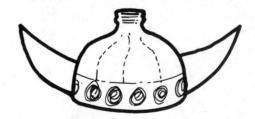

Victor's **V** Words

V

v

van

vacuum

volcano

vase

Victor Viking

by _____

Victor Viking is very venturesome.

2

1

venturesome

vest

7

village

volleyball

8

He is always victorious.

6

He wears a violet velvet vest.

5

He plays volleyball.

3

He plays for the Village Vikings.

4

Special Activities for *Ww*

Introduce the sound of the week, using the Winnie Witch puppet (see *Bagging It with Puppets!*), and present the Winnie Witch chart story (page 140).

Music

"Winnie Witch" (page 145).

Language Arts

Books:

Adams, Adrienne. *A Woggle of Witches.* New York: Scribner, 1971.

Allard, Harry. *Miss Nelson Is Missing.* Boston: Houghton Mifflin, 1977.

Balian, Lorna. *Humbug Witch.* Nashville, TN: Abingdon Press, 1965.

Watson, Jane Werner. *Which Is the Witch?* New York: Pantheon, 1979.

Poetry:

Fylman, Rose. "Witch, Witch." In *Treasure Chest of Poetry,* pg. 38. Allen, Texas: DLM Teaching Resources, 1986.

Magee, Wes. "The Witch's Brew." In *A Very First Poetry Book,* pg. 98. New York: Oxford University Press, 1984.

Moore, Lilian. "Listen!" In *A New Treasure of Children's Poetry,* pg. 168. New York: Doubleday, 1984.

Resnikoff, Alexander. "Two Witches." In *The Random House Book of Poetry for Children,* pg. 190. New York: Random House, 1983.

Cooking

Winnie Witch's Wacky Waffles (page 158).

Handwriting

Silly sentence: Winnie Witch wears weird wigs.

Give each child a copy of Winnie's *W* Words (page 81).

Art

Give each child two colors of the same-size paper to make a woven mat. Have children cut one sheet of paper into lengthwise strips. Have them fold the other sheet in half lengthwise, and starting at the fold, cut slits across the paper, stopping about an inch from the edge. Children unfold the paper and weave the strips in and out of the slits. Glue the ends of the strips in place.

Something Special

Teach the children the song "Witches' Brew" (*Witches' Brew,* by Hap and Martha Palmer, Educational Activities, Inc., P.O. Box 392, Freeport, New York 11520). This is a wonderful song for movement activities. After the children know the song, they can think of new things to put in the witch's brew. Great for language development, too. Try making some witch's brew in class!

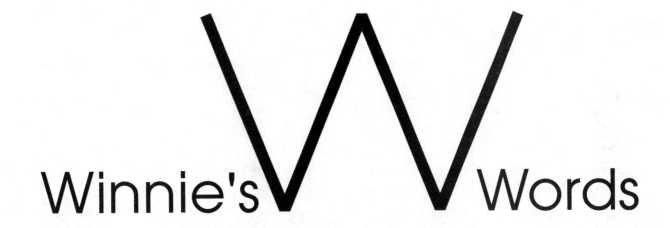

Winnie's W Words

W

w

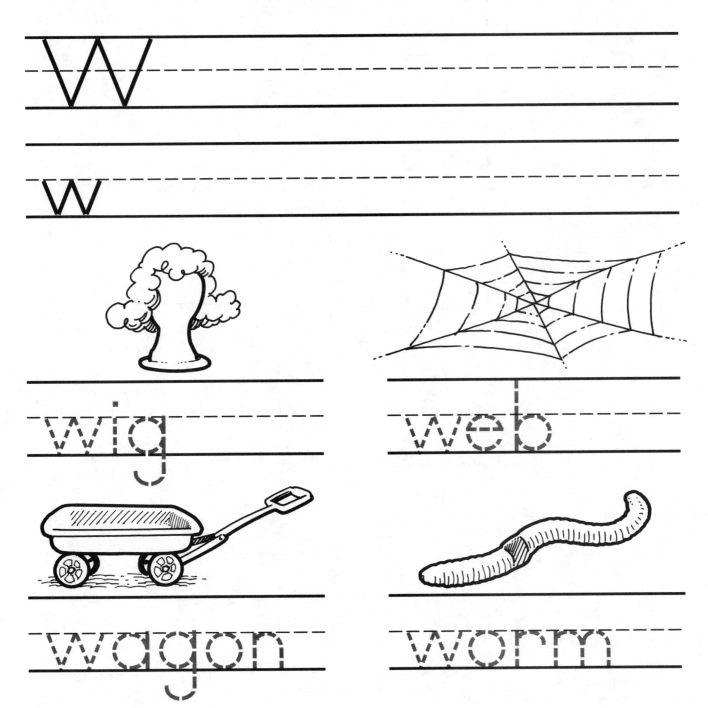

wig

web

wagon

worm

Winnie Witch

by

_____

Winnie Witch is weird.

2

1

weird

wild

7

_____

8

night

rides

She has a wacky hat.

3

Her hair is wild and woolly.

4

Her broom at night she rides.

5

Wee-ee-ee-ee!

6

Special Activities for *Xx*

> Introduce the sound of the week, using the X-Ray Boy puppet (see *Bagging It with Puppets!*), and present the X-Ray Boy chart story (page 140).

Music

"X-Ray Boy" (page 145).

Language Arts

Books:
Felder, Eleanore. *X Marks the Spot.*
  New York: Coward-McCann, 1972.
Hefter, Richard. *Xerus Won't Allow It.*
  New York: Holt, 1978.

Poetry:
  In all the alphabet a letter that
    will vex,
  Is the one near the end, called
    the letter X,
  There aren't many words that
    start with this sound,
  In the dictionary only a few was
    all that I found.

Cooking

X-Ray Boy's Maxi-Mix (page 159).

Handwriting

Silly sentence: X-Ray Boy examines xylophones.

  Give each child a copy of X-Ray Boy's *X* Words (page 85).

Science/Math

Draw a skeleton of a person or animal on a large sheet of butcher paper. On tagboard, make all the bones necessary to reconstruct the skeleton. Write a number problem on each bone. Children solve the problems, match the body parts, and attach them to the skeleton.

  Contact a doctor, dentist, or veterinarian to bring in different types of X-rays. Let children examine them and try to identify problems.

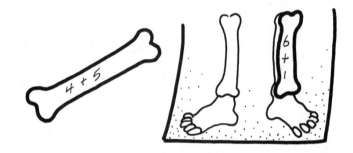

Art

Children can use clean chicken bones to make skeleton pictures on white construction paper. They can make hands, rib cages, arms, or any other body parts. Spray over the bones with black paint and then remove the bones when the paint is dry. (Spray inside a cardboard box in a well-ventilated area.) Voila! You will have X-ray pictures!

X-Ray Boy's X Words

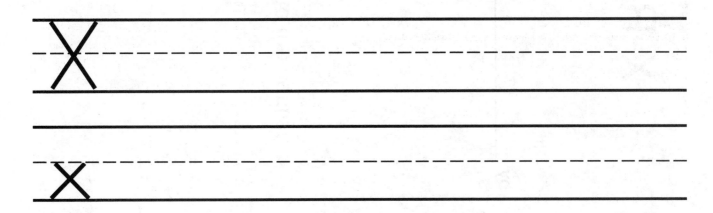

X

x

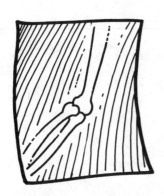

exercise

x-ray

X-Ray Boy

X-Ray Boy goes to the dentist.

2

1

by

_____

teeth

home

box

fix

7

8

He brought it home in a box.

6

Maxine, the dentist, X-rays his teeth.

3

5

4

"I will fix it."

"Oh, no! You have a loose tooth."

Special Activities for *Yy*

> Introduce the sound of the week, using the Yakky Yak puppet (see *Bagging It with Puppets!*), and present the Yakky Yak chart story (page 140).

Music

"Yakky Yak" (page 145).

Language Arts

Books:
Hefter, Richard. *Yakety Yak Yak Yak.* New York: Holt, 1977.

Lawson, Annetta. *The Lucky Yak.* Boston: Houghton Mifflin, 1980.

Stamaty, Mark Alan. *Yellow, Yellow.* New York: McGraw-Hill, 1971.

Poetry:
Hymes, Lucia, and James Hymes, Jr. "My Favorite Word." In *Poems Children Will Sit Still For,* pg. 75. New York: Scholastic Book Services, 1969.

McCord, David. "Yellow." In *The Random House Book of Poetry for Children,* pg. 220. New York: Random House, 1983.

Ross, David. "A Yak." In *Treasure Chest of Poetry,* pg. 92. Allen, Texas: DLM Teaching Resources, 1986.

Smith, William. "Yak." In *The Golden Treasury of Poetry,* pg. 55. New York: Golden Press, 1957.

Cooking

Yakky Yak's Yummy Yogurt Pops (page 159).

Handwriting

Silly sentence: Yakky Yak yanks yellow yo-yos.

Give each child a copy of Yakky's *Y* Words (page 89).

Art

Children can make yarn designs on construction paper. Have the children draw the line designs on their papers first and then spread glue on the lines. After spreading the glue, the students place pieces of yarn over it. Or, have children stitch with yellow yarn on pieces of burlap!

Math

Cut pieces of yellow yarn several different lengths. Have children estimate how long each piece is. Then, measure with a yardstick to see who guessed most accurately.

Something Special

Visit a yak at the local zoo.

Have the class bring yo-yos to school to share.

Yakky's Y Words

Y

y

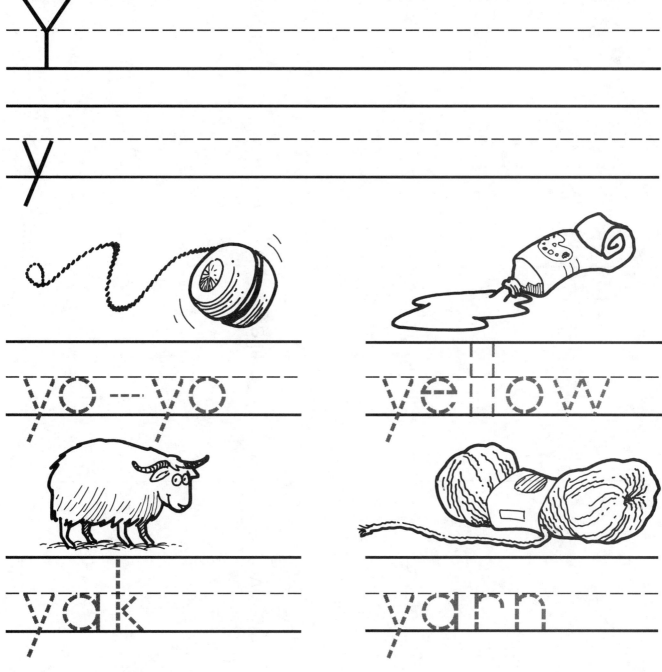

yo-yo

yellow

yak

yarn

Yakky Yak

by _____

Yakky Yak is yelling.

2

1

Words from Our Story

yelling

yellow

7

8

yo-yo

broken

His yellow yarn has broken.

3

Oh! Oh! Oh!

6

Yank, yank, yank.

4

The yellow yo-yo won't go.

5

Special Activities for *Zz*

Introduce the sound of the week, using the Zeke Zebra puppet (see *Bagging It with Puppets!*), and present the Zeke Zebra chart story (page 140).

Music

"Zeke and Zelda" (page 145).

Language Arts

Books:

Carle, Eric. *1, 2, 3, to the Zoo.* Cleveland, Ohio: Collins-World, 1969.

Hadithi, Mwenye. *Greedy Zebra.* Boston: Little, Brown, 1984.

Massie, Diane Redfield. *Zigger Beans.* New York: Parents' Magazine Press, 1971.

Seuss, Dr. *On Beyond Zebra.* New York: Random House, 1955.

Poetry:

Bissett, Donald J. "The Zebra." In *Poems and Verses about Animals,* Book 2, pg. 45. Novato, CA: Chandler & Sharp Publishers, 1967.

Prelutsky, Jack. "The Zebra." In *Zoo Doings,* pg. 60. New York: Greenwillow Books, 1970.

Silverstein, Shel. "Zebra Question." In *A Light in the Attic,* pg. 125. New York: Harper & Row, 1981.

Cooking

Zeke's Zippy Zonkers (page 159).

Handwriting

Silly sentence: Zeke Zebra zaps zinnias. Give each child a copy of Zeke's *Z* Words (page 93).

Math

Draw a garden plot on a large piece of butcher paper. Cut zinnias from tagboard. Write a number problem in the center of each flower. Students can either "pick" or "plant" the zinnias.

Science

Have each child plant and care for a zinnia garden. Be sure to plant different varieties, so children will realize that all zinnias are not the same size, shape, or color.

Art

Read the poem "The Zebra" before children begin this zany zebra mural. Then, each student can draw a large zebra on 18" x 24" construction paper or have a pattern available to trace. Children can paint the zebras plaid, checked, spotted, or covered with polka dots!

Zeke's Z Words

Z

z

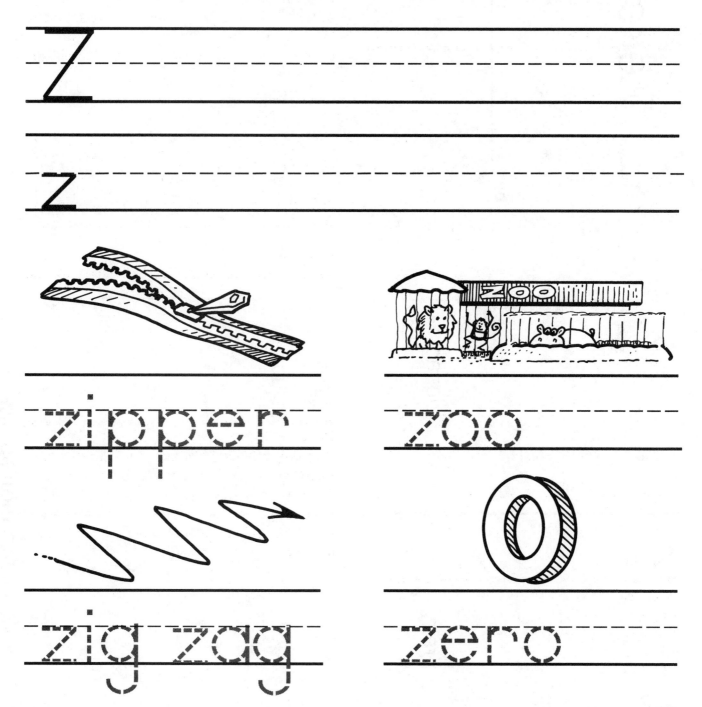

zipper   zoo

zig zag   zero

Zeke Zebra

by _____

Zeke and Zelda Zebra lived at the zoo.

2

1

Words from Our Story

zinnias   zoo

7

zigzag   pretty

8

Through the pretty zinnias.

6

Zigzag, zigzag, zigzag!

5

They grew pretty zinnias.

3

They had to zig and zag.

4

Special Activities for Short *Aa*

Introduce the sound of the week, using the Astronaut Andy or Astronaut Annie puppets (see *Bagging It with Puppets!*), and present the Astronaut Annie chart story (page 138).

Music

"The Astronauts are Here" (page 146).

Language Arts

Books:

Moche, Dinal L. *The Astronauts.* New York: Random House, 1979.

Slobodkin, Louis. *Space Ship Under the Apple Tree.* New York: Vanguard Press Inc., 1952.

———. *Space Ship Returns to the Apple Tree.* New York: Vanguard Press, Inc., 1958.

Wildsmith, Brian. *Professor Noah's Spaceship,* New York: Oxford University Press, 1980.

Zacks, Irene. *Space Alphabet.* Englewood Cliffs, NJ: Prentice-Hall, 1964.

Poetry:

Dodson, Fitzhugh, Dr. "Spaceman, Spaceman!" In *I Wish I Had a Computer that Makes Waffles,* pg. 49. San Diego, CA: Oak Tree Publications, Inc., 1978.

Foster, John. "Let's Send a Rocket." In *A Very First Poetry Book,* pg. 44. New York: Oxford University Press, 1979.

———. "Space Spot." In *A Very First Poetry Book,* pg. 36. New York: Oxford University Press, 1979.

Cooking

Annie's Astronomical Applesauce (page 148).

Handwriting

Silly sentence: Annie Astronaut advertises applesauce.

Give each child a copy of Annie's *A* Words (page 97).

Science/Math

Count how many objects in the classroom begin with the short *A* sound and make a graph to show the results. (If you have a class of 26 students, you should find at least 54 ankles!)

Children can build a space center, using Legos or other building materials.

Make and launch rockets. (Be sure children do this with adult supervision.)

Art

Provide the book *Easy to Make Spaceships that Really Fly,* by Mary Blocksma (Prentice-Hall, 1983). Allow children to "research" and then make spaceships.

Children can create a space mural, using tempera paint.

Children can make space dioramas from shoe boxes.

Something Special

Show a space film (available through NASA).

Eat astronaut food available through: American Outdoor Products, Inc.
1540 Charles Drive
Redding, CA 96003

Annie's 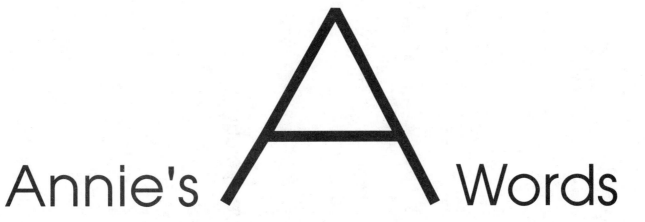 Words

A

a

accident

ant

apple

ax

Astronaut Annie

by

_____

Annie is an astronaut.

2

1

astronaut

accident

ambulance

ankle

7

8

Er-r-r-r! Off goes Annie.

6

An ambulance came for Annie.

5

Annie had an accident.

3

Annie hurt her ankle.

4

Special Activities for Short *Ee*

> Introduce the sound of the week, using the Ellie Elephant puppet (see *Bagging It with Puppets!*), and present the Ellie Elephant chart story (page 138).

Music

"Ellie Is an Elephant" (page 146).

Language Arts

Books:

Hoff, Syd. *Oliver.* New York: Harper & Row, 1960.

McKee, David. *Elmer, the Story of a Patchwork Elephant.* New York: McGraw-Hill, 1968.

Peet, Bill. *Ella.* Boston: Houghton Mifflin, 1964.

Samson, Ann S. *Draw Me an Elephant.* New York: Doubleday, 1967.

Wahl, Jan. *Hello Elephant.* New York: Holt, 1964.

Poetry:

Becker, Edna. "Beside the Line of Elephants." In *The Random House Book of Poetry for Children,* pg. 59. New York: Random House, 1983.

Link, Lenore M. "Holding Hands." In *The Random House Book of Poetry for Children,* pg. 58. New York: Random House, 1983.

McGinley, Phyllis. "E is the Escalator." In *Away We Go,* pg. 22. New York: Crowell, 1956.

Richards, Laura E. "Eletelephony." In *A Treasure of Children's Poetry,* pg. 102. New York: Doubleday, 1984.

Cooking

Ellie's Elegant Eggs (page 150).

Handwriting

Silly sentence: Ellie Elephant exits elevators elegantly.

Give each child a copy of Ellie's *E* Words (page 101).

Science/Math

Bring in different types of eggs (turkey, duck, fish, snake). Let children compare size, shape, and texture.

Art

Each student can draw (or have a pattern available to trace) a large elephant on 18" x 24" construction paper. Children can use pebbles, toothpicks, fabric scraps, sponge paint, tempera paint, torn paper, or wallpaper to make designs on the elephants.

Give each child two elephant patterns reproduced on gray construction paper to cut out. Put the two shapes together and staple all around the edges, leaving one side open. Let the children stuff the elephants with cotton and then staple the final side closed.

Ellie's E Words

E

e

EXIT

exit

eggs

elephant

Ellie Elephant

by

_____

Ellie is a BIG elephant.

2

1

big

long

four

short

7

8

Ellie has four BIG feet.

6

Ellie has a SHORT tail.

5

Ellie has BIG ears.

3

Ellie has a LONG trunk.

4

Special Activities for Short *Ii*

> Introduce the sound of the week, using the Ill Izzy puppet (see *Bagging It with Puppets!*), and present the Ill Izzy chart story (page 138).

Music

"Izzy Is Ill" (page 146).

Language Arts

Books:

Charlip, Remy. *Mother, Mother I Feel Sick*. New York: Parents, 1966.

Cobb, Vicki. *How the Doctor Knows You're Fine*. Philadelphia, PA: Lippincott, 1973.

Lerner, Marguerite Rush. *Dear Little Mumps Child*. Minneapolis, MN: Lerner, 1959.

Overlie, George. *Michael Gets the Measles*. Minneapolis, MN: Lerner, 1959.

———. *Peter Gets the Chickenpox*. Minneapolis, MN: Lerner, 1959.

Rockwell, Anne F. *Sick in Bed*. New York: Macmillan, 1982.

Poetry:

Lee, Dennis. "Doctor, Doctor." In *Jelly Belly*, pg. 37. London: Blantyre Printing and Binding Ltd., 1983.

Cooking

Izzy's Instantly Incredible Puddings (page 152).

Handwriting

Silly sentence: Ill Izzy is in intensive care. Give each child a copy of Izzy's *I* Words (page 105).

Science/Math

Bring in different types of thermometers and discuss their uses with the children. Children can learn to read the degree marks, counting by twos and tens.

Art

Children can each make a giant thermometer to record every day's temperature. Reproduce a thermometer pattern on tagboard for children to cut out and label with degree increments. Use elastic to represent the mercury. Color part of it red and slit the tagboard so that the elastic will move easily.

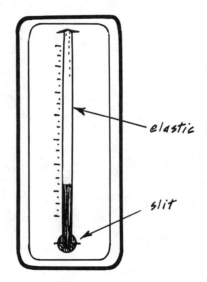

elastic

slit

Izzy's I Words

I

i

igloo

insect

inside

invite

Words from Our Story

Poor Izzy is ill.

Izzy III III

2

1

by

hot

7

sad

bed

8

play

Izzy cannot go out to play.

6

Mom put him to bed.

3

Izzy is sad.

5

Izzy feels hot.

4

Special Activities for Short Oo

Introduce the sound of the week, using the Ollie Octopus puppet (see *Bagging It with Puppets!*), and present the Ollie Octopus chart story (page 139).

Music

"Ollie Is an Octopus" (page 146).

Language Arts

Books:

Barrett, John. *Oscar the Selfish Octopus.* New York: Human Sciences Press, Inc., 1978.

Carrick, Carol. *Octopus.* New York: Seabury Press, 1978.

Most, Bernard. *My Very Own Octopus.* San Diego, CA: Harcourt Brace Jovanovich, 1980.

Ungerer, Tomi. *Emile.* New York: Harper & Row, 1960.

Waber, Bernard. *I Was All Thumbs.* Boston: Houghton Mifflin, 1975.

Poetry:

Nash, Ogden. "The Octopus." In *The Sound of Poetry,* pg. 119. Newton, MA: Allyn and Bacon, 1963.

Starkey, Richard. "Octopus's Garden." In *Silver Burdett Music,* Book 1. Morristown, NJ: Silver Burdett and Ginn, 1981.

Cooking

Ollie Octopus's Ominous Omelet (page 154).

Handwriting

Silly sentence: Ollie Octopus offers omelets.

Give each child a copy of Ollie's *O* Words (page 109).

Art/Science

Combine your study of short *O* with a study of the octopus.

Something Special

Take a field trip to an aquarium or zoo where children can see a live octopus!

Ollie's 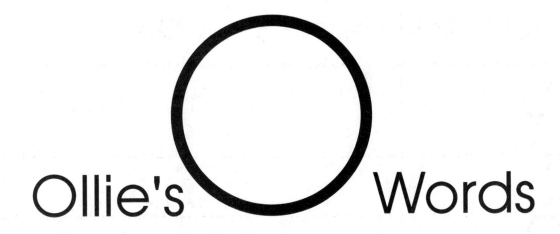 Words

O

o

omelet

ostrich

octopus

otter

Ollie Octopus

by _____

Ollie is an octopus.

2

1

_____

octopus 7 eight

swim 8 under

Swish, swish, swish!

6

See his eight long arms go.

5

Ollie lives under the water.

3

Ollie can swim fast.

4

Special Activities for Short *Uu*

Introduce the sound of the week, using the Uncle Sam puppet (see *Bagging It with Puppets!*), and present the Uncle Sam chart story (page 140).

Music

"Uncle Sam" (page 146).

Language Arts

Books:
Berkley, Ethel. *Ups and Down*. Reading, MA: Addison-Wesley, 1951.

Blance, Ellen. *Monster and the Magic Umbrella*. Los Angeles, CA: Bowmar, 1973.

Bright, Robert. *My Red Umbrella*. New York: Morrow, 1959.

Johnson, Crockett. *Upside Down*. Niles, IL: Albert Whitman, 1969.

Yashima, Taro. *Umbrella*. New York: Viking, 1958.

Poetry:
McCune, Ann. "Red, White, and Blue." In *Poetry Place Anthology,* pg. 98. New York: Instructor Books, 1983.

Graham, Harry, "Uncle." In *The Random House Book of Poetry for Children,* pg. 159. New York: Random House, 1983.

Cooking

Uncle Sam's Upside-Down Cake (page 157).

Handwriting

Silly sentence: Uncle Sam unpacks umbrellas.

Give each child a copy of Uncle Sam's *U* Words (page 113).

Art

Have each child cover a toilet tissue roll with red or blue construction paper and decorate the roll with white or silver stick-on stars. Cut 1/2" x 5" red, white, or blue crepe paper strips and give several to each student to glue on the bottom of the roll. Punch two holes at the top of each role for students to attach a piece of yarn. Students can hang their "unsocks" and watch them fly in the breeze.

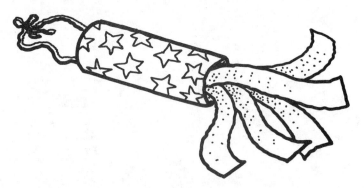

Math

Have children find out how many uncles they have. Make a graph showing who has the most, the least, or the same amount as another classmate. How many uncles all together?

Uncle Sam's U Words

U

u

uncle

us

umbrella

up

Uncle Sam

by _____

This is Uncle Sam.

2

1

Words from Our Story

tall

coat

7

white

hat

8

Hurrah for Uncle Sam!

6

His coat is blue.

See his tall hat.

3

It is red, white, and blue.

4

5

Special Activities for Long *Aa*

> Introduce the sound of the week, using the Amy Angel puppet (see *Bagging It with Puppets!*), and present the Amy Angel chart story (page 138).

Music

"Amy Angel" (page 147).

Language Arts

Books:

Anderson, Hans Christian. *The Red Shoes*. Natick, MA: Alphabet Press, 1983.

Benet, William Rose. *Angels*. New York: Crowell, 1947.

Kavanaugh, James J. *The Crooked Angel*. Los Angeles, CA: Nash, 1970.

Krahn, Fernando. *A Funny Friend from Heaven*. Philadelphia, PA: Lippincott, 1977.

Ness, Evaline. *Marcella's Guardian Angel*. New York: Holiday House, 1979.

Poetry:

Amy's an angel who likes angel cake.
She knows letter *A* is easy to make.
She plays on a harp all made of gold,
And sings letter *A* songs to both young
and old.
(G. Mehrens)

Cooking

Amy Angel's Angel Wings (page 148).

Handwriting

Silly sentence: Amy Angel ate angel cake.
Give each child a copy of Amy's *A* Words (page 117).

Art

Children can make fingerprints on small white notecards with black or blue stamp pads. They can use a fine point marker to add details to make tiny "angel" creations. Children can tie a ribbon around five notecards and envelopes to give as a present to someone special.

Math

Teach the South Carolina folk song "The Angel Band" (*36 South Carolina Spirituals,* by Carl Diton, G. Schirmer, Inc., 1950, 1957). It is excellent for practicing numerals 1 through 10.

Amy's A Words

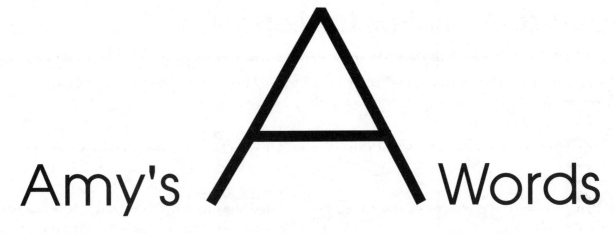

A

a

apron   ace

angel   acorn

Amy Angel

by

_____

Amy is an angel.

2

1

angel

7

pretty

sing

8

play

Words from Our Story

Amy likes to eat angel food cake.

6

Amy likes to play.

5

Amy Angel is pretty.

3

Amy likes to sing.

4

Special Activities for Long *Ee*

> Introduce the sound of the week, using the Edith Eagle puppet (see *Bagging It with Puppets!*), and present the Edith Eagle chart story (page 138).

Music

"Edith Eagle" (page 147).

Language Arts

Books:

Adrian, Mary. *The American Eagle.* New York: Hastings House, 1963.

Benchley, Nathaniel. *Running Owl, the Hunter.* New York: Harper & Row, 1979.

Climo, Shirley. *King of the Birds.* New York: Crowell, 1988.

Foreman, Michael. *Moose.* New York: Pantheon, 1972.

Sharmat, Mitchell. *Reddy Rattler and Easy Eagle.* New York: Doubleday, 1979.

Poetry:

Gardner, John. "The Eagle." In *A Child's Bestiary,* pg. 18. New York: Knopf, 1977.

Tennyson, Alfred. "The Eagle." In *Favorite Poem's Old and New,* pg. 291. New York: Doubleday, 1957.

Record:

Palmer, Hap, and Martha Palmer. "The Eagle." *Witches' Brew.* Educational Activities, Inc., Box 392, Freeport, NY 11520.

Cooking

Edith Eagle's Easy Eclairs (page 149).

Handwriting

Silly sentence: Edith Eagle eats enormous eclairs.

Give each child a copy of Edith's *E* Words (page 121).

Art

Draw and cut out several large *E*'s on 18" x 24" pieces of tagboard for children to use as patterns. Have each child trace and cut out an *E* on an 18" x 24" piece of colored construction paper. Children can decorate the *E*'s with scraps of paper, tissue, or fabric. Make a tube for each child by rolling an 18" x 24" piece of construction paper diagonally around a pencil. Drop the pencil out and tape the roll in place. Tape each child's *E* to a tube and have an *E* parade!

Math

Discuss the word *enormous*. Brainstorm things that are ENORMOUS and make a list or class book.

Edith's E Words

E
e

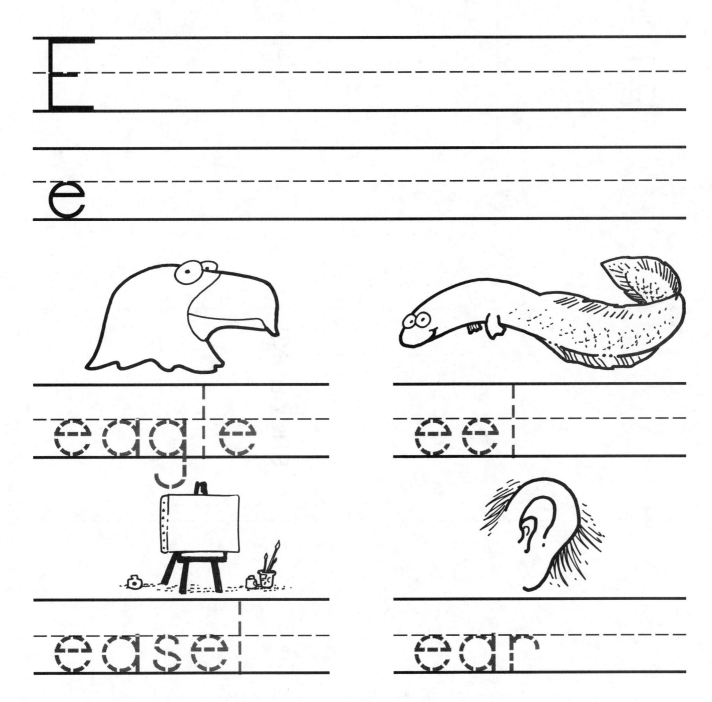

eagle

eel

ease

ear

Edith Eagle

by

_____

This is Edith Eagle.

2

1

ENORMOUS

7

sharp

claws

8

fly

See her fly high up in the sky.

6

Edith has sharp claws.

3

Edith has ENORMOUS wings.

5

Edith has an ENORMOUS beak.

4

Special Activities for Long *Ii*

> Introduce the sound of the week, using the Ice-Cream Ike puppet (see *Bagging It with Puppets!*), and present the Ice-Cream Ike chart story (page 139).

Music

"Ike, the Ice-Cream Man" (page 147).

Language Arts

Books:

Armitage, Ronda. *Ice Cream for Rosie.* New York: Elsevier-Dutton, 1981.

Hunwitz, Johanna. *Aldo Ice Cream.* New York: Morrow, 1981.

Lexau, Joan. *Striped Ice Cream.* Philadelphia, PA: Lippincott, 1968.

Rayner, Mary. *Garth Pig and the Ice Cream Lady.* New York: Atheneum, 1977.

Testa, Fulvio. *The Land Where the Ice Cream Grows.* New York: Doubleday, 1979.

Poetry:

Archambault, John. "Ice Cream." In *Treasure Chest of Poetry,* pg. 185. Allen, Texas: DLM Teaching Resources, 1986.

Field, Rachel. "The Ice Cream Man." In *Treasure Chest of Poetry,* pg. 185. Allen, Texas: DLM Teaching Resources, 1986.

Hubbard, Alice. "The Ice Cream Man." In *Golden Flute,* pg. 249. New York: John Day & Co., 1932.

Silverstein, Shel. "Eighteen Flavors." In *Where the Sidewalk Ends,* pg. 116. New York: Harper & Row, 1974.

Cooking

Ike's Ice Cream (page 152).

Handwriting

Silly sentence: Ice-Cream Ike isolates icicles.

Give each child a copy of Ike's *I* Words (page 125).

Art

Provide brown construction paper for ice-cream cones, an assortment of colored construction paper for ice-cream scoops, and 5" x 24" strips of white construction paper for children to create ice-cream cone pictures.

Math

Count how many scoops of ice cream each child has on his or her cone from the art project and graph the results. Or, make a graph of the children's favorite ice-cream flavors.

Something Special

Go on a field trip to an ice-cream parlor and order ice-cream cones or sundaes!

Ike's I Words

I

i

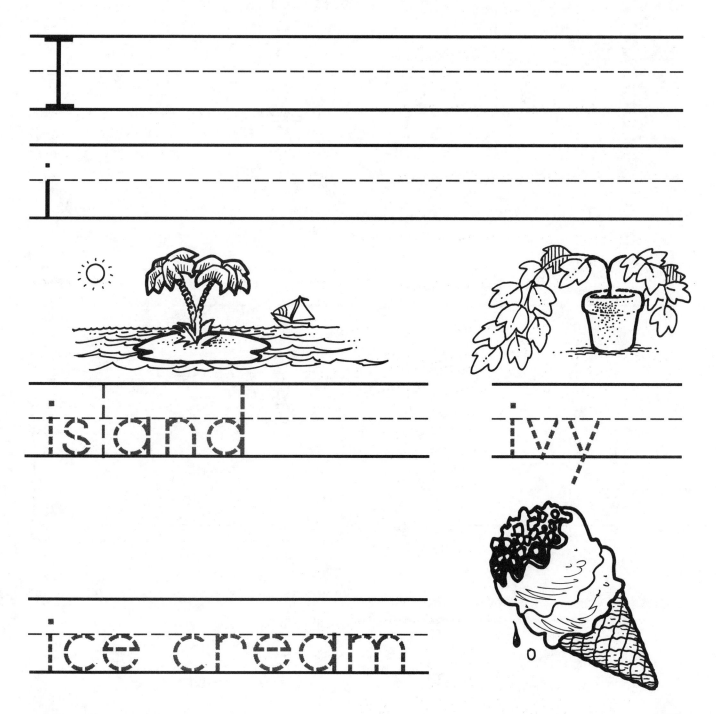

island

ivy

ice cream

Ice-Cream Ike

by _____

"Ice Cream! Ice Cream!" calls Ike.

2

1

happy

up

ice cream

7

8

down

Yum! Yum! Yum!

6

Ice cream for you and me.

Ike is the happy ice-cream man.

3

All the boys and girls jump up and down.

4

Special Activities for Long *Oo*

> Introduce the sound of the week, using the Ogie Ogre puppet (see *Bagging It with Puppets!*), and present the Ogie Ogre chart story (page 139).

Music

"Ogie Ogre" (page 147).

Language Arts

Books:

Gackenback, Dick. *Harry and the Terrible Whatzit*. New York: Seabury, 1977.

Ginsburg, Mirra. *Ookie-Spooky*. New York: Crown, 1979.

Mayer, Mercer. *There's a Nightmare in My Closet*. New York: Dial Press, 1968.

Stevens, Kathleen. *Beast in the Bathtub*. Milwaukee, Wisconsin: Colony Pre Press, 1983.

Ungerer, Tomi. *Zeraldas Ogre*. New York: Harper & Row, 1967.

Poetry:

Prelutsky, Jack. "The Ogre." In *Nightmares,* pg. 24. New York: Greenwillow, 1976.

Thompson, Dorothy. "Shreiks at Midnight." In *Shreiks at Midnight,* pg. 1. New York: Crowell, 1969.

Cooking

Ogie Ogre's Oatmeal Cookies (page 154).

Handwriting

Silly sentence: Ogie Ogre owns overshoes. Give each child a copy of Ogie's *O* Words (page 129).

Science/Math

Use colored construction paper to make stepping stones and write a math problem on each stone. Place the stones on the classroom floor to make a path to "Ogie's Place." Choose a child to be Ogie. Have children follow the path by solving each math problem. If a mistake is made, Ogie takes that child to his or her hideaway.

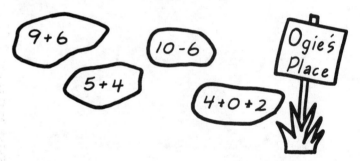

Art

Children can make papier-mâché monster masks. Grease an upside-down bowl, pie tin, or cake tin with petroleum jelly for each child. Have children cover bowls with strips of newspaper dipped in liquid starch. Eyes, noses, ears, and wrinkles can be made by gluing on string, pieces of egg carton, and cardboard. Children cover over the glued additions with two more layers of newspaper strips dipped in starch. Allow masks to dry and remove them from the bowls. Paint the masks and add hair.

Ogie's O Words

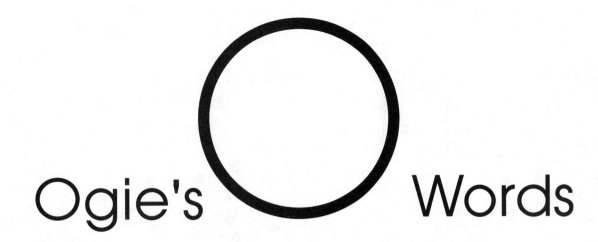

O _ _ _ _ _ _ _ _ _ _ _ _ _ _ _ _ _ _

o _ _ _ _ _ _ _ _ _ _ _ _ _ _ _ _ _ _

oatmeal

old

overshoes

It's All in the Bag! © 1990 Fearon Teacher Aids

Ogie Ogre

by _____

Ogie is an ogre.

2

1

ugly

7

mean

little

8

green

Oh! Oh! Oh!

6

But he's not very mean.

5

He is little and green.

3

Ogie is very ugly.

4

Special Activities for Long *Uu*

> Introduce the sound of the week, using the Una Unicorn puppet (see *Bagging It with Puppets!*), and present the Una Unicorn chart story (page 140).

Music

"Una the Unicorn" (page 147).

Language Arts

Books:
Cooper, Glae. *Unicorn Moon.* New York: Dutton, 1984.
Coville, Bruce. *Sarah's Unicorn.* Philadelphia, PA: Lippincott, 1979.
Mayer, Marianna. *The Unicorn and the Lake.* New York: Dial Press, 1982.
Razzi, Jim. *Fun with Unicorns.* New York: Scholastic, 1987.

Poetry:
Cromwell, Liz. "The Unicorn." In *Finger Frolics,* pg. 104. Luonia, Michigan: Partner Press, 1983.
Silverstein, Shel. "The Unicorn." In *The Random House Book of Poetry for Children,* pg. 209. New York: Random House, 1983.
Smith, William Jay. "Unicorn." In *The Random House Book of Poetry for Children,* pg. 209. New York: Random House, 1983.

Cooking

Una Unicorn's Unique Banana Horns (page 157).

Handwriting

Silly sentence: Una Unicorn usually uses uniforms.

Give each child a copy of Una's *U* Words (page 133).

Math/Language

Explain to children that a unicorn is a mythical animal that resembles a horse, with one horn in the middle of its forehead. Explain that the prefix *uni* means *one* and discuss words containing the prefix:

unicolor—of only one color
unidirectional—moving in only one direction
uniform—always the same
unicycle—vehicle having a single wheel
unique—one and only
unite—to bring together, make one

Social Studies

Discuss why community helpers and other people wear uniforms. Make a classroom book of people who wear uniforms.

Art

Each child can make a small ukulele from an empty matchbox and a tongue depressor. Cut a hole in the top of each box for the children. Children string wire or rubber bands across the hole and secure them with brads. The children can then decorate the boxes and play unique tunes!

Una's U Words

U

u

unicorn

utensils

ukulele

unicycle

Una Unicorn

by _____

I love unicorns!

2

1

love

7

long

purple

8

horn

I love Una unicorn.

6

Una has a long horn.

Una is a unicorn.

3

Una is a pretty, purple unicorn.

4

Part Two: Resources

chart stories
songs
recipes

Chart Stories

Astronaut Annie

Annie is an astronaut.
Annie had an accident.
Annie hurt her ankle.
An ambulance came for Annie.
Er-r-r-r! Off goes Annie!

Amy Angel

Amy is an angel.
Amy Angel is pretty.
Amy likes to sing.
Amy likes to play.
Amy likes to eat angel food cake.

Billy Boy

"Boo-hoo-hoo," said Billy Boy.
"I had a new bat."
"I had a new ball."
"I broke the bat."
"I lost the ball! Boo-hoo-hoo!"

Cowboy Curly

"Yippee-i-yay!" said Cowboy Curly.
"I can ride a horse."
"I can rope a calf."
"I sit by the fire."
"I play my guitar."

Doctor Donna

See Doctor Donna.
See her nurse, Dot.
Dot is dizzy.
Help! Doctor Donna!
Help dizzy Dot!

Edith Eagle

This is Edith Eagle.
Edith has sharp claws.
Edith has an ENORMOUS beak.
Edith has ENORMOUS wings.
See her fly high up in the sky.

Ellie Elephant

Ellie is a BIG elephant.
Ellie has BIG ears.
Ellie has a LONG trunk.
Ellie has a SHORT tail.
Ellie has four BIG feet.

Firefighter Fred

Here is Firefighter Fred.
Here is Fred's dog, Fritz.
Here is Fred's fire truck.
Er-r-r-r! Fire! Fire! Fire!
Here go Fred and Fritz to fight the fire.

Greta Girl

"Grumble, grumble, grumble," groans
   Greta.
"I can't find my green galoshes."
"I can't find my gray glove."
"I can't find my gold gown."
"But I can find my gooey gumdrops!"

Harry Hippopotamus

Hop! Hop! Hop! goes Harry
   Hippopotamus.
First on one foot.
Then on two.
Hopping to the hippo market.
Hot dogs for you!

Ill Izzy

Poor Izzy is ill.
Mom put him to bed.
Izzy feels hot.
Izzy is sad.
Izzy cannot go out to play.

Chart Stories

Ice-Cream Ike

"Ice Cream! Ice Cream!" calls Ike.
Ike is the happy ice-cream man.
All the boys and girls jump up and down.
Ice cream for you and me.
Yum! Yum! Yum!

Jack-in-the-Box

Jump! Jump! Jump! goes Jack.
Up and down, up and down.
Like a very happy clown.
Oh! Oh! Oh!
Back down you go.

Kooky Kookaburra

Kooky Kookaburra goes to Kindergarten.
Mrs. King is the teacher.
Kooky keeps time to the music.
Klip-klop, klip-klop.
At recess, Kooky flies kites.

Lionel Lion

Lionel Lion loves lollipops.
Big ones, little ones, round ones, too.
Red ones, green ones,
Lemon ones, too!
Yum! Yum! Yum!

Merry Mouse

"M-m-m-m-m!" said Merry Mouse.
"I will make some mud pies."
"I will make many, many mud pies."
"I will make a mess!"
"I will make a merry, merry mess!"

Nurse Nancy

Nurse Nancy eats nachos.
Nurse Nancy eats nuts.
Nurse Nancy eats noodles.
Nurse Nancy eats nectarines.
Morning, noon, and night!

Ollie Octopus

Ollie is an octopus.
Ollie lives under the water.
Ollie can swim fast.
See his eight long arms go.
Swish, swish, swish!

Ogie Ogre

Ogie is an ogre.
He is little and green.
Ogie is very ugly.
But he's not very mean.
Oh! Oh! Oh!

Peter Pig

Peter Pig pops popcorn.
Piles and piles of popcorn.
Pink and purple and puffy.
Pop! Pop! Pop!
Popcorn popping. Pop! Pop! Pop!

Queenie Queen

Queenie Queen likes to quilt.
She quilts quickly and quietly.
She gets a quarter per quilt.
Poor Queenie.
Maybe she should quit!

Randy Robot

See Randy Robot.
See Randy Robot run.
See Randy Robot run to the red racer.
Go Randy! Go! Go! Go!
See Randy's racer go fast!

Silly Scarecrow

Can you see Silly Scarecrow?
Silly Scarecrow looks funny.
See its funny hat.
See its funny jacket.
See its funny pants.

Chart Stories

Tanya Tiger

"Rr-r-r," said Tanya Tiger.
"I can jump over a puddle."
"I can run in the grass."
"I can climb a tree."
"I can hide in a bush."

Una Unicorn

I love unicorns!
Una is a unicorn.
Una is a pretty, purple unicorn.
Una has a long horn.
I love Una Unicorn.

Uncle Sam

This is Uncle Sam.
See his tall hat.
It is red, white, and blue.
His coat is blue.
Hurrah for Uncle Sam!

Victor Viking

Victor Viking is very venturesome.
He plays volleyball.
He plays for the Village Vikings.
He wears a violet velvet vest.
He is always victorious.

Winnie Witch

Winnie Witch is weird.
She has a wacky hat.
Her hair is wild and woolly.
Her broom at night she rides.
Wee-ee-ee-ee!

X-Ray Boy

X-Ray Boy goes to the dentist.
Maxine, the dentist, x-rays his teeth.
"Oh, no. You have a loose tooth."
"I will fix it."
He brought it home in a box.

Yakky Yak

Yakky Yak is yelling.
His yellow yarn has broken.
Yank, yank, yank.
The yellow yo-yo won't go.
Oh! Oh! Oh!

Zeke Zebra

Zeke and Zelda Zebra lived at the zoo.
They grew pretty zinnias.
They had to zig and zag.
Zigzag, zigzag, zigzag!
Through the pretty zinnias.

Songs

Did You Ever See a Robot?

(Sing to the tune of "Did You Ever See a Lassie?")

Did you ever see a robot, a robot, a robot?
Did you ever see a robot go this way and that?
Go forward and backward,
And backward and forward.
Did you ever see a robot go this way and that?

Repeat the song and substitute the bold lines with the following:

With arms up and arms down,
And arms down and arms up.
or
With leg up and leg down,
And leg down and leg up.

(Make new verses using different robot actions.)

Silly Scarecrow

(Sing to the tune of "Alouette.")

Chorus:
Silly Scarecrow, silly, silly scarecrow
Silly Scarecrow, flapping in the breeze.

Verse 1:
See its very funny hat.
See its very funny hat.
Funny hat.
Funny hat.
Oh . . . (repeat chorus)

Verse 2:
See its very funny jacket.
See its very funny jacket.
Funny jacket.
Funny jacket.
Funny hat.
Funny hat.
Oh . . . (repeat chorus)

Verse 3:
See its very funny pants.
See its very funny pants.
Funny pants.
Funny pants.
Funny jacket.
Funny jacket.
Funny hat.
Funny hat.
Oh . . . (repeat chorus)

Songs

Tanya Tiger

(Sing to the tune of "John Brown's
    Body.")

Tanya Tiger has stripes upon her back.
Tanya Tiger has stripes upon her back.
Tanya Tiger has stripes upon her back.
Gr-gr-gr-gr-grrr!
(Add your own verses!)

Merry Mouse

(Sing to the tune of "Are You Sleeping?")

Merry Mouse, Merry Mouse,
You're a mess, you're a mess.
Making many mud pies,
Making many mud pies,
Mother will be sad,
Mother will be sad!

Merry Mouse, Merry Mouse
Clean up your mess, clean up your mess.
No more messy mud pies,
No more messy mud pies.
Mother will be glad,
Mother will be glad.

Did You Ever Meet a Firefighter?

(Sing to the tune of "Did You Ever See a
    Lassie?")

Did you ever meet a firefighter, a
    firefighter, a firefighter?
Did you ever meet a firefighter with a dog
    named Fritz?
Fights fires, helps people, climbs
    ladders up steeples.
Did you ever meet a firefighter with a dog
    named Fritz?

Billy Boy, Billy Boy

(Sing to the tune of "Billy Boy, Billy Boy.")

Oh, where is your ball
Billy Boy, Billy Boy.
Oh, where is your ball
Baseball Billy.

I threw it far and high,
way up in the sky.
And now I cannot find it.

B-I-L-L-Y

(Sing to the tune of "Bingo")

There was a boy who had a ball and Billy
    was his name, oh,
B-I-L-L-Y, B-I-L-L-Y, B-I-L-L-Y,
    and Billy was his name, oh!

Cowboy Curly

(Sing to the tune of "Battle Hymn of the
    Republic.")

My name is Cowboy Curly, and I ride
    upon a horse.
My name is Cowboy Curly, and I ride
    upon a horse.
My name is Cowboy Curly, and I ride
    upon a horse.
Yippee-yi, Yippee-yo, Yippee-ya.

Verse 2:
My name is Cowboy Curly, and I can
    rope a calf . . .

Verse 3:
My name is Cowboy Curly, and I play an
    old guitar . . .

Songs

Doctor Donna

(Sing to the tune of "Are You Sleeping?")

Doctor Donna, Doctor Donna,
I am sick, I am sick,
This is an emergency,
This is an emergency,
Quick! Quick! Quick!
Quick! Quick! Quick!

Greta Girl

Chant:
Greta Girl, Greta Girl
Snap, snap, snap!
Greta Girl, Greta Girl
Tap, tap, tap!
Greta Girl, Greta Girl
Clap, clap, clap!
Greta Girl, Greta Girl
Touch your lap.

Harry Hippo

(Sing to the tune of "Skip to My Lou.")

Harry Hippo, hop, hop, hop.
Harry Hippo, hop, hop, hop.
Harry Hippo, hop, hop, hop.
Hop to the hippo market.

First on one foot, then on two.
First on one foot, then on two.
First on one foot, then on two.
Hop to the hippo market.

Buying hot dogs 1, 2, 3.
Buying hot dogs 1, 2, 3.
Buying hot dogs 1, 2, 3.
Oh, how good they'll be.

Jack is Jumping Up and Down

(Sing to the tune of "London Bridge.")

Jack is jumping up and down, up and
    down, up and down.
Jack is jumping up and down, like a
    happy clown.

See his head go in and out, in and out, in
    and out.
See his head go in and out, hear the
    children shout.

Lionel the Lion

(Sing to the tune of "Battle Hymn of the
    Republic.")

Li-o-nel the lion likes to lick his lollipops,
Li-o-nel the lion likes to lick his lollipops,
Li-o-nel the lion likes to lick his lollipops,
Yum, Yum, Yum, Yum, Yum, Yum!

Big ones, little ones, round ones, too,
Big ones, little ones, round ones, too,
Big ones, little ones, round ones, too,
Yum, Yum, Yum, Yum, Yum, Yum!

Red ones, green ones, lemon ones, too,
Red ones, green ones, lemon ones, too,
Red ones, green ones, lemon ones, too,
Yum, Yum, Yum, Yum, Yum, Yum!

Songs

N-A-N-C-Y

(Sing to the tune of "Bingo.")

There was a school,
It had a nurse.
And Nancy was her name, oh!
N-A-N-C-Y
N-A-N-C-Y
N-A-N-C-Y
And Nancy was her name, oh!

Verse 2: *-A-N-C-Y
Verse 3: *-*-N-C-Y
Verse 4: *-*-*-C-Y
Verse 5: *-*-*-*-Y
Verse 6: *-*-*-*-*
(Clap on each *)

All the Kookaburras

(Sing to the tune of "Down by the Station.")

All the Kookaburras go to kindergarten,
Mrs. King, the teacher, teaches them to sing.
Hear the Kookaburras making pretty music,
La-la, la-la, hear them sing.

Popping Popcorn

(Sing to the tune of "London Bridge.")

Popping popcorn is such fun,
Is such fun, is such fun.
Popping popcorn is such fun,
Yum-Yum, Yum! Yum! Yum!

Did You Ever Eat a Pizza?

(Sing to the tune of "Did You Ever See a Lassie?")

Did you ever eat a pizza, a pizza, a pizza,
Did you ever eat a pizza
So big, fat, and round?

Queenie Queen

(Sing to the tune of "Deep in the Heart of Texas.")

Oh, Queenie Queen is tall and lean (clap, clap, clap),
Here in the halls of (name of school).
Her hair is gold,
She's not too old (clap, clap, clap),
Here in the halls of (name of school).
She likes to read,
And does good deeds (clap, clap, clap),
Here in the halls of (name of school).

Victor Viking

(Sing to the tune of "Clementine.")

Victor Viking, Victor Viking
Wears a violet velvet vest.
He is vigorous, he is venturesome,
He is always victorious!

Songs

Winnie Witch

(Sing to the tune of "Hambone Chant.")

Winnie Witch, Winnie Witch, pots a
  boilin'.
Winnie Witch, Winnie Witch, hinges need
  oilin'.
Winnie Witch, Winnie Witch, broom can
  fly.
Winnie Witch, Winnie Witch, up in the
  sky.

  Alternate clapping hands and clapping
hands on knees while chanting the first
two lines.
  Alternate clapping hands and clapping
hands on thighs while chanting the last
two lines.

X-Ray Boy

(Sing to the tune of "Frere Jacques.")

X-Ray Boy, X-Ray Boy,
How are you? How are you?
My tooth is very loose.
My tooth is very loose.
X-ray it! X-ray it!

X-Ray Boy, X-Ray Boy
It is very loose, it is very loose,
We've got to pull it out,
We've got to pull it out.
It won't hurt. It won't hurt.

Yakky Yak

(Sing to the tune of "London Bridge.")

Yakky Yak is yell-ing, yell-ing, yell-ing,
Yakky Yak is yell-ing,
His yo-yo is broken.

Fix it up with yellow yarn, yellow yarn,
  yellow yarn,
Fix it up with yellow yarn,
And stop your yelling.

See it going up and down, up and down,
  up and down,
See it going up and down,
It's not bro-ken.

Zeke and Zelda

(Sing to the tune of "Funiculi, Funicula.")

Zeke and Zelda live in a zoo.
Growing zinnias,
All for me and you,
For me and you, for me and you,
For me and you, for me and you.
Growing pretty zinnias,
All for me and you.

Songs

The Astronauts Are Here

(Sing to the tune of "The Farmer in the
   Dell.")

The astronauts are here.
The astronauts are here.
Walking in their spacesuits
And all their other gear.

(Make up your own verses!)

Ellie Is an Elephant

(Sing to the tune of "Here We Go 'round
   the Mulberry Bush.")

Ellie is an elephant,
Elephant, elephant.
Ellie is an elephant,
Who lives at the zoo.

This is the way she swings her trunk,
Swings her trunk, swings her trunk.
This is the way she swings her trunk,
When she wants to play.

(Add your own verses!)

Izzy Is Ill

(Sing to the tune of "Jimmy Crack Corn.")

Izzy is ill, give him a pill,
Izzy is ill, give him a pill,
Izzy is ill, give him a pill,
And he'll get better today.

Put'm in bed, he feels so hot,
Put'm in bed, he feels so hot,
Put'm in bed, he feels so hot,
And he'll get better today.

Izzy is sad, he cannot play,
Izzy is sad, he cannot play,
Izzy is sad, he cannot play,
But he'll get better today!

Ollie Is an Octopus

(Sing to the tune of "When Johnny Comes
Marching Home Again.")

Oh, Ollie is an octopus
Swish-swish, swish-swish.
Oh, Ollie is an octopus
Swish-swish, swish-swish.
He lives in the water and swims around,
His eight long arms never touch the
   ground,
And we'll all swim fast when Ollie comes
   around!

Uncle Sam

(Sing to the tune of "Battle Hymn of the
   Republic.")

This is my friend and his name is Uncle
   Sam,
This is my friend and his name is Uncle
   Sam,
This is my friend and his name is Uncle
   Sam,
And his hat is red, white, and blue.

Uncle Sam's hat is very, very tall,
Uncle Sam's hat is very, very tall,
Uncle Sam's hat is very, very tall,
And it's colored red, white, and blue.

Songs

Amy Angel

(Sing to the tune of "Clementine.")

Amy Angel, Amy Angel
Playing on her golden harp.
She is singing, she is playing,
While she's eating angel cake.

She plays fast, she plays slow,
She plays wherever she goes.
Making music, pretty music,
While she's eating angel cake.

Edith Eagle

(Sing to the tune of "Mary Had a Little Lamb.")

Edith Eagle has sharp claws,
Has sharp claws, has sharp claws.
Edith eagle has sharp claws,
And ENORMOUS wings.

See her fly in the sky,
In the sky, in the sky.
See her fly in the sky,
On ENORMOUS wings.

See her huge, ENORMOUS beak,
ENORMOUS beak, ENORMOUS beak.
See her huge, ENORMOUS beak,
And ENORMOUS wings.

Ike, the Ice-Cream Man

(Sing to the tune of "Here We Go 'round the Mulberry Bush.")

Here comes Ike, the ice-cream man,
Ice-cream man, ice-cream man.
Here comes Ike, the ice-cream man,
With treats for you and me!

Chocolate, strawberry, lemon, too,
Maple nut and raspberry goo,
Bubble gum and melon dew,
They're treats for you and me!

Ogie Ogre

(Sing to the tune of "Frere Jacques.")

Ogie Ogre, Ogie Ogre
Little and green, little and green.
He is very ugly, he is very ugly
He looks weird, he looks weird.

Una the Unicorn

(Sing to the tune of "Mary Had a Little Lamb.")

I love a u-ni-corn,
U-ni-corn, u-ni-corn.
I love a u-ni-corn,
And Una is her name.

She's a purple u-ni-corn,
U-ni-corn, u-ni-corn.
She's a purple u-ni-corn,
And Una is her name.

She-e has a long, long horn,
Long, long horn, long, long horn.
She-e has a long, long horn,
And Una is her name.

Recipes

Amy Angel's Angel Wings

1 can water chestnuts (cut in half)
soy sauce
sugar
bacon

Marinate water chestnuts in soy sauce for at least one hour. Roll each water chestnut in sugar and wrap with 1/2 slice of bacon. Secure with a toothpick. Bake at 350° F for 15 minutes. Then broil for 3 minutes.
(Serves 10)

Annie's Astronomical Applesauce

15 large apples
3 cups sugar
6 cups water
cinnamon (optional)

Combine sugar and water in an electric pot. Bring to a boil. Peel and chop apples and add them to the boiling syrup. Cook until soft. Whip, add cinnamon, and cool. Enjoy!
(Serves 25–30)

Billy Boy's Best Burgers

lean ground beef
hamburger buns (1 per child)
salt
pepper

Measure 1/3 cup portions of ground beef and shape into oval patties. Fry in a nonstick skillet. Season with salt and pepper. Arrange platter with lettuce, tomatoes, cheese slices, relish, pickles, catsup, mayonnaise, and hamburger buns.

Recipes

Cowboy Curly's Crunchy Candy

2 tablespoons margarine
1 (6 oz.) package chocolate chips
1 1/2 cups crunchy peanut butter
36 large marshmallows

Arrange marshmallows in an 8" x 8" pan in rows of 6. Melt margarine over low heat in a heavy saucepan or double boiler. Add chocolate chips and peanut butter and stir until melted and blended. Pour mixture over marshmallows and refrigerate until firm. When ready to serve, let stand at room temperature for 10 minutes. Cut between marshmallows and serve.
(Makes 3 dozen)

Doctor Dan's Divine Peanut Butter Play Dough

1 cup powdered milk
1/2 cup peanut butter
1/4 cup honey

Combine all ingredients and mix well. Children can mold sculptures and then eat their creations. The dough does not keep well, so make only as much as needed.
(Serves 3)

Edith Eagle's Easy Eclairs

whipped topping
chocolate bars
soda crackers

Spread whipped topping over soda crackers. Top with a section of chocolate bar. Add another dab of whipped topping and cover with another soda cracker.

Recipes

Ellie's Elegant Eggs

1/2 cup margarine
1 teaspoon vanilla
sugar
12 ounces semisweet chocolate morsels
decorating sprinkles

Cream margarine and vanilla. Gradually add sugar (one tablespoon at a time) until a stiff mixture forms. Divide into teaspoon-size balls and shape into eggs between palms. Chill in a waxed paper-lined container. Melt chocolate morsels. Use a fork to dip eggs into melted chocolate. Decorate eggs with sprinkles. Makes about 25–30 eggs.

Firefighter Fred's Fantastic Fudgesicles

1 (4 oz.) package instant chocolate pudding mix
2 cups milk
1/4 cup sugar
1 cup canned evaporated milk

Combine pudding mix and 2 cups milk in a large mixing bowl. Beat two minutes. Stir in sugar and canned milk. Pour into popsicle molds and freeze.
(Serves 18)

Recipes

Greta Girl's Granola

1/4 cup butter
1/4 cup honey
1 1/2 teaspoon cinnamon
1/2 teaspoon salt
1 cup flaked coconut
1 cup chopped nuts
3 cups quick-cooking rolled oats

Preheat oven to 350° F. Melt butter in a 13" x 9" baking pan. Stir honey into the melted butter and add all remaining ingredients, mixing thoroughly. Spread evenly in pan. Bake for about 30 minutes or until lightly browned and crispy. Keep an eye on the mixture during baking, stirring occasionally to prevent burning. When cool, store in a tightly covered container. Serve as a cold cereal, snack, or yummy ice-cream topping.

Harry Hippo's Happy Hot Dogs

1 hot dog (split in half lengthwise)
2 slices bread
1 slice cheese
mayonnaise
catsup
butter

Preheat oven to 400° F. Make a cheese sandwich. Cut it into a round shape, using a cutter. Wrap the sandwich around a hot dog and fasten it with toothpicks. Place on a greased cookie sheet. Brush bread and hot dog with butter. Let child create a face on the hot dog with catsup from a squeeze dispenser. Bake for 5 minutes.
(Serves 1)

Recipes

Ike's Ice Cream

4 beaten eggs
2 cups sugar
4 tablespoons vanilla
pinch of salt
2 cups heavy cream
10 cups milk

Mix all ingredients in a 1-gallon ice cream freezer and
freeze.
(Serves 25–30)

Izzy's Instantly Incredible Puddings

variety of instant puddings
whipped topping
chopped nuts
maraschino cherries

Follow directions on pudding packages. Pour pudding into
small paper or clear plastic cups. Garnish with whipped
topping. Sprinkle with chopped nuts and sliced maraschino cherries.

Jack-in-the-Box Juicesicles

1 (6 oz.) can frozen orange juice concentrate
1 juice can of cold water
1 egg white
2 tablespoons honey

Mix all ingredients together in a blender. Pour the
blended juice into paper cups or plastic popsicle cups and
freeze. If using paper cups, let the mixture become semi-
frozen before inserting sticks. When ready to serve, run
the plastic popsicle cups under tap water to make removal
easier.
(Serves 6–12)

Recipes

Kooky's Kohlrabi Dip

1/4 cup yogurt
1/2 teaspoon lemon juice
1/2 teaspoon dry Italian salad dressing mix
kohlrabi

Mix all ingredients together well. Serve with cutup kohl-rabi.

Lionel Lion's Luscious Lemonade

1 (6 oz.) can frozen lemonade concentrate
1 (6 oz.) can frozen orange juice concentrate
4 cups water
2 cups vanilla ice cream

Combine all ingredients in blender. Blend on medium speed until mixed and foamy.
(Makes 7 1/2 cups)

Merry Mouse's Marvelous Muffins

1 (8 1/2 oz.) corn muffin mix
1/3 cup crushed pineapple (reserve 1/4 cup juice)
1 egg

Drain pineapple and measure 1/4 cup juice. Combine muffin mix, crushed pineapple, pineapple juice, and egg. Stir until just moistened. Spoon into paper muffin cups and bake at 400° F for 15–20 minutes or until golden brown.
(Serves 6–8)

Recipes

Nancy Nurse's Nifty Nachos

tortilla chips
grated cheddar cheese
chopped olives

Preheat oven to 400° F. Place chips on a cookie sheet in a single layer. Sprinkle with cheese. Top with olives. Bake in hot oven until bubbly.

Ogie Ogre's Oatmeal Cookies

1 cup oatmeal
1 cup crunchy peanut butter
1 cup honey
1 cup dry milk
1 cup raisins

Put all ingredients into a large bowl and mix well. Roll into 1-tablespoon balls. Do not cook!
(Serves 25–30)

Ollie Octopus's Ominous Omelet

3 eggs
1/2 teaspoon salt
1/4 teaspoon pepper
1 teaspoon water
1 tablespoon butter

Blend first four ingredients in a blender and slowly heat a 9" nonstick skillet. Melt butter in skillet and pour in blended mixture. As eggs begin to set, add your choice of filling (cheese, mushrooms, bacon bits, ham, green pepper). Pull edges of egg mixture slightly up toward the center to let the uncooked egg flow onto the hot skillet. Remove from skillet when completely cooked and enjoy!
(Serves 3)

Recipes

Peter Pig's Purple Punch

1 (6 oz.) can frozen grape juice concentrate
1 cup low fat milk
2 cups vanilla ice cream

Blend juice concentrate and milk. Add ice cream and blend on high speed. Makes about one quart. Serve immediately. (Serves 12)

Queenie Queen's Quick Quencher

1 package orange drink mix
1 cup sugar
1 gallon water
1 (12 oz.) can frozen orange juice
1 (12 oz.) can frozen pineapple juice
1 (12 oz.) can frozen lemonade

Mix all ingredients together in a large bowl and serve. (Serves 25–30)

Randy Robot's Racy Raisin Ripple

2 (13 oz.) cans Eagle Brand condensed milk
1 (13 oz.) can evaporated milk
1 (12 oz.) package chocolate chips (crushed in blender)
1 cup raisins
2 tablespoons vanilla
milk

Combine the first five ingredients in a homemade ice-cream freezer. Add milk to fill container. Freeze according to directions on freezer. Serve in small paper cups. (Serves 25–30)

Recipes

Silly Scarecrow's Scrumptious Skillet Spaghetti

1 lb. lean ground beef
1 (1 1/2 oz.) package dry spaghetti sauce mix
1 (8 oz.) can tomato sauce
1 1/2 cups water
12 ounces spaghetti noodles (cooked)
parmesan cheese

Brown ground beef in skillet and drain. Stir in spaghetti sauce mix, tomato sauce, and water. Cook over medium heat until heated through. Add cooked spaghetti and toss to coat. Serve with parmesan cheese.
(Serves 4–6)

Tanya Tiger's Terrific Twists

1 (12 oz.) package canned refrigerator biscuits
softened butter
1/3 cup sugar
1 teaspoon cinnamon
1/2 cup sifted powdered sugar
water

Separate biscuits and flatten each one into a 4" circle. Spread each circle with about a teaspoon of butter. Combine sugar and cinnamon. Sprinkle evenly over circles. Cut circles in half, place buttered sides together and twist. Place on cookie sheet and bake at 400° F for 10–12 minutes or until golden brown. Combine powdered sugar and water to make a glaze. Drizzle over warm cinnamon twists.
(Serves 10)

Recipes

Una Unicorn's Unique Banana Horns

6 ripe bananas (peeled)
12 wooden sticks
1 cup semisweet chocolate morsels
1 tablespoon butter

Cut bananas in half. Insert a stick at one end of each banana half and freeze. Melt chocolate morsels and butter in the top of a double boiler. When bananas are frozen, dip each into the chocolate mixture. When the cold has glazed the chocolate, wrap each banana in aluminum foil and store in freezer until ready to serve.
(Serves 12)

Uncle Sam's Upside-Down Cake

2 tablespoons melted butter
2 tablespoons brown sugar
1 can (1 lb. 8 oz.) cherry pie filling
yellow cake mix

Put melted butter and brown sugar in the bottom of a 9" square pan. Pour cherry pie filling over the mixture. Prepare cake mix according to directions on package. Spread batter over cherry filling. Bake for 35–45 minutes at temperature suggested on cake mix package. Remove from oven and cool 5 minutes. Turn upside down on plate so that fruit makes a topping on the cake. Serve warm with ice cream or whipped cream.
(Serves 8–10)

Recipes

Victor's Vegetable Soup

4 cups water
3 large carrots
3 potatoes
3 onions
2 stalks celery
1 (16 oz.) can tomatoes
1 (16 oz.) can corn
1 (16 oz.) can peas
4 teaspoons beef bouillon
dash of salt

Heat water in a large pot. Peel and cut up carrots, potatoes, onions, and celery. Boil these ingredients until soft. Add bouillon, tomatoes, corn, and peas (do not drain). Add salt and boil 10 minutes. Serve in small paper cups with crackers.
(Serves 25–30)

Winnie Witch's Wacky Waffles

pancake or waffle mix
whipped cream in a squirt can
blueberries
strawberries

Prepare waffles according to directions on package. Make wacky faces on waffles, using whipped cream in a squirt can. Use blueberries for eyes and a strawberry for a nose. Let your imagination go wild!

Recipes

X-Ray Boy's Maxi-Mix

2 tablespoons raisins
2 tablespoons peanuts
2 tablespoons granola

Mix well.
(Serves 1)

Yakky Yak's Yummy Yogurt Pops

1 cup fresh strawberries (hulled and sliced) or any fruit
1/4 cup honey
2 cups plain yogurt
6 (6 oz.) paper cups
6 wooden sticks

Combine strawberries, yogurt, and honey in bowl or
blender. Put mixture into small paper cups and freeze for 20
minutes. Add sticks. Freeze until firm. Peel off paper cups
before eating.
(Serves 6)

Zeke's Zippy Zonkers

1 (6 oz.) package butterscotch chips
1/4 cup crunchy peanut butter
3 1/2 cups cornflakes

Melt butterscotch chips and peanut butter over low heat in
heavy saucepan. Stir in cornflakes and mix well. Drop from
spoon onto waxed paper.
(Serves 25–30)